T0043637

LIFE
IS 10%
WHAT HAPPENS TO YOU AND
90%
HOW YOU REACT

LIFE
IS 10%
WHAT HAPPENS TO YOU AND
90%
HOW YOU REACT

CHARLES SWINDOLL

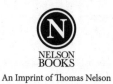

NELSON
BOOKS

An Imprint of Thomas Nelson

Life Is 10% What Happens to You and 90% How You React

© 1992, 1994, 2023 Charles Swindoll

Portions of this book were adapted from *Active Spirituality* and *Laugh Again.*

All rights reserved. No portion of this book may be reproduced, stored in a retrieval system, or transmitted in any form or by any means—electronic, mechanical, photocopy, recording, scanning, or other—except for brief quotations in critical reviews or articles, without the prior written permission of the publisher.

Published in Nashville, Tennessee, by Nelson Books, an imprint of Thomas Nelson. Nelson Books and Thomas Nelson are registered trademarks of HarperCollins Christian Publishing, Inc.

Thomas Nelson titles may be purchased in bulk for educational, business, fundraising, or sales promotional use. For information, please e-mail SpecialMarkets@ThomasNelson.com.

Unless otherwise noted, Scripture quotations are taken from the New American Standard Bible® (NASB). Copyright © 1960, 1962, 1963, 1968, 1971, 1973, 1975, 1977, 1995 by The Lockman Foundation. Used by permission. www. Lockman.org.

Scripture quotations marked KJV are taken from the King James Version. Public domain.

Scripture quotations taken from the Holy Bible, New International Version®, NIV®. Copyright © 1973, 1978, 1984, 2011 by Biblica, Inc.® Used by permission of Zondervan. All rights reserved worldwide. www.Zondervan.com. The "NIV" and "New International Version" are trademarks registered in the United States Patent and Trademark Office by Biblica, Inc.®

Scripture quotations marked TLB are taken from The Living Bible. Copyright © 1971. Used by permission of Tyndale House Publishers, a Division of Tyndale House Ministries, Carol Stream, Illinois 60188. All rights reserved.

ISBN 978-1-4003-3343-1 (audiobook)
ISBN 978-1-4003-3342-4 (eBook)
ISBN 978-1-4003-3327-1 (paperback)

Library of Congress Cataloging-in-Publication Data

Duplicate to LCCN : 2022022618

Printed in the United States of America

23 24 25 26 27 LBC 6 5 4 3 2

CONTENTS

INTRODUCTION

THE LONGER I LIVE, THE MORE I REALIZE THE impact of attitude on life. Attitude, to me, is more important than the past, than education, than money, than circumstances. Attitude is more important than failures and successes. More important than what other people think or say or do. It's more important than appearance, giftedness, or skill. Attitude will make or break a company, a church, and a home.

And attitude will make or break your life.

The remarkable thing is we have a choice every day regarding the attitude we will embrace. We can't change our past. We can't change the fact that people will treat us a certain way. We can't change the inevitable. The only thing we can do is play on the one string we have, and that's our attitude. I am convinced that life is 10 percent what happens to you and 90 percent how you react.

And so it is with you.

Growing up, I'm sure more than once your parent, mentor, or teacher told you, "Attitude is everything!" Well, it's not everything, but I'm convinced it's almost everything. Attitude is a way of thinking and feeling, yes, but it's also a way of acting. Your attitude is so powerful that it can be seen in your nonverbal behavior. Nonverbal communication plays a big role in your life. It can improve your ability to relate, engage, and establish meaningful, authentic interactions every day.

Every waking moment of our lives we operate from one of two viewpoints: human or divine. I often refer to these as "the horizontal perspective" and "the vertical perspective." The more popular of the two is human; it's also the easiest because it comes so naturally. The more fruitful of the two is divine; yet it's hard to lift our eyes from the horizontal, to extricate ourselves from the mundane. I don't know about you, but I often catch myself wanting to think my own thoughts, keep my own attitudes, and lead my own life independently of God's perspective.

Though all of us struggle to spread our wings of faith and rise above the horizontal perspective, none of us has the same journey or life experiences. There's no one else like you in the entire world. Never has been, never will be. We all deal with different challenges and tragedies—

- disappointment in ourselves and others
- betrayal by people we trusted
- abuse or neglect by those who should have protected and provided

- debilitating illness or disfiguring injuries
- unmet expectations and shattered dreams
- lost livelihood

The list could go on and on . . . and on. In fact, the longer we live in this broken world, that list will grow.

Yet even amid troubles like these, each of us has the same moment-by-moment choice. We can either unfurl the white flag of surrender and allow the bad things to roll over us like a column of tanks . . . or we can dig in our heels, stand our ground, and put up a fight. How? It's all about how you react. It's about the attitude you decide to embrace.

This reminds me of an episode in my own life several years ago. Across the room in my study hung an original oil painting illuminated by the golden glow of a light. My mother gave me that painting many years after I entered the ministry. She painted it herself. In brilliant colors it portrays a shepherd surrounded by a handful of sheep on a green hillside.

Though I had stared at that painting countless times, that day something struck me. In the bottom right corner, I looked at the date—just days before she passed into the Lord's presence. Caught in that nostalgia, I turned off my desk lamp and stared at the painting. There I sat, thanking God anew for my mother's prayers, my pilgrimage, and especially God's presence. Faithfully, graciously, quietly He had led me and helped me and blessed me. I bowed my head and thanked Him for His sustaining grace. I began to weep with gratitude . . . and with a tinge of melancholy that comes when we hold our breath and dive deeply into the depths of our past.

Suddenly the shrill sound of the telephone broke the silence, pulling me into the present. My youngest son, Chuck, was on the line wanting to tell me something funny that had happened. I abruptly switched gears and enjoyed one of those delightful, lighthearted father-son moments. As we laughed loudly together, he urged me to hurry home.

What an attitude adjustment! Following his call, I paused beside the painting once again, and this time I thought of the significant role my parents had played in those formative years of my life. Now the torch had been passed on from them to my wife, Cynthia, and me to do the same with our sons and daughters . . . and they, in turn, with theirs.

In moments like those, we must choose to move forward.

Yes, we should acknowledge the past with its pains and joys, sorrows and successes. But we don't drown in the past; we draw from it. It's a choice. We either choose to look backwards and aimlessly drift in a sea of sadness . . . or we choose to appreciate the blessings and to paddle forward with an attitude of optimism that can affect generations to come.

I'm not saying what happens to you won't hurt. It often will. I'm not saying you shouldn't take your feelings seriously. You should. What I am saying is your every-moment decisions have momentous consequences for the future.

———

I wrote *Laugh Again* and *Active Spirituality* many years ago. The world has changed a lot since then, and I've often wondered how I could reach others and provide them with a resource to improve their mental, emotional, and spiritual health in a world increasingly toxic toward life-promoting attitudes. I realized that much wisdom was in those two books, but it needed to be bridged together and updated. It needed to meet people where they are today. And that wisdom needed to be lined with grace and mercy for an increasingly graceless and merciless world.

This book is a result of that labor.

We are all on a quest, but you're the only person who

can choose how you'll react to what life throws at you. This book will guide you through the process of resolving life's dilemmas. It'll teach you how to free yourself from constant drama. It'll help you achieve and maintain balance. And it'll remind you how to have a joyous and fruitful life.

Because life isn't simply about what happens to you . . . it's about how you react.

CHAPTER 1

FINDING JOY

THIS CHAPTER IS ALL ABOUT JOY.

It's about relaxing more, releasing the tension, and refusing to let circumstances spoil our attitudes.

It's about looking at life from a perspective other than today's traffic report, social media post, or evening news.

It's about giving the child within us permission to look at life and laugh again.

Can you remember when life was joyful? I certainly can. Without any knowledge of the Dow index or the drop in the gross domestic product or the accelerating crime rate in America or the decreasing healthcare benefits in our country's major companies, I was happy as a clam. I neither expected much nor needed much. Life was meant to be enjoyed, not endured, and every day I found something—anything—to laugh about.

One of my favorite true stories about finding joy in the unexpected makes me smile every time I think about it.

Grandmother and granddaughter, a very precocious ten-year-old, were spending the evening together when the little girl suddenly looked up and asked, "How old are you, Grandma?"

3

The question startled the woman, but knowing her granddaughter's quick little mind, she wasn't completely shocked.

"Well, honey, when you're my age you don't share your age with anybody."

"Aw, go ahead, Grandma . . . you can trust me."

"No, dear, I never tell anyone my age."

Grandmother got busy fixing supper, then she suddenly realized the little darling had been absent for about twenty minutes—much too long! She checked around upstairs in her bedroom and found that her granddaughter had dumped the contents of her grandmother's purse on top of her bed and was sitting in the midst of the mess, holding her grandmother's driver's license.

When their eyes met, the child announced, "Grandma, you're seventy-six."

"Why, yes, I am. How did you know that?"

"I found the date of your birthday here on your driver's license and subtracted that year from this year . . . so you're seventy-six!"

"That's right, sweetheart. Your grandmother is seventy-six."

The little girl continued staring at the driver's license and added, "You also made an F in sex, Grandma."

Sometime between that age of childhood innocence

4

and right now, life has become a grim marathon of frowns—a major downer for far too many adults. I suppose some would justify the change by saying, "When you become an adult, you need to be responsible." I couldn't agree more. My question is this: When did a healthy, well-exercised sense of humor get sacrificed on the altar of adulthood? Who says becoming a responsible adult means a long face and an all-serious attitude toward life?

My vocation is among the most serious of all professions. As a minister of the gospel and senior pastor of a church, the concerns I deal with are eternal in scope. A week doesn't pass without dealing with life in the raw. Marriages are breaking, homes are splitting, people are hurting, jobs are dissolving, addictions of every description are rampant. Needs are enormous, endless, and heartrending.

Tough times are upon us, no question. The issues we all face are both serious and real. But are they so intense, so all-important, so serious, and so all-consuming that every expression of joy should be eclipsed? Sorry, I can't buy that.

A good sense of humor enlivens our discernment and guards us from taking everything that comes down the pike too seriously. By remaining lighthearted, by refusing to allow our intensity to gain the mastery of our minds, we remain much more objective. People who live above their circumstances usually possess a well-developed sense of humor, because in the final analysis that's what gets them through.

Finding joy in the mundane and challenging seasons is the key to living a balanced life. There will always be times when we don't think we'll make it, but if we're willing to hold on to joy and relish in those moments, we'll identify better ways to handle life.

THE DEEP NEED FOR JOY

I know of no greater need today than the need for joy. Unexplainable, contagious joy. Outrageous joy.

When that kind of joy comes aboard our ship of life, it brings good things with it—like enthusiasm for life, determination to hang in there, and a strong desire to be an encouragement to others. Such qualities make our voyage bearable when we hit the open seas and encounter high waves of hardship that tend to demoralize and paralyze. A joyful attitude will help us sail through wave after wave of the challenges life sends our way.

Someone once asked Mother Teresa what the job

description was for anyone who wanted to work alongside her in the grimy streets and narrow alleys of Calcutta.
Without hesitation she mentioned only two things: the
desire to work hard and a joyful attitude. It has been my
observation that both of those qualities are rare. But the
second is much rarer than the first. Diligence may be difficult to find, but compared to an attitude of genuine joy,
hard work is commonplace.

Unfortunately, our world seems to have lost its spirit
of fun and laughter. Just look around. Bad news, long
faces, and heavy hearts are everywhere—even in houses
of worship. Much of today's popular music promotes
misery, revenge, sorrow, and despair. If sex and violence
are not the pulsating themes of a new film or TV series,
some expression of unhappiness is. Media outlets and
social media newsfeeds thrive on tragedies and calamities, lost jobs, and horrible accidents. Even the weather
reports give their primary attention to storms, droughts,
and blizzards. Tomorrow is usually "partly cloudy with a
20 percent chance of rain," never "mostly clear with an
80 percent chance of sunshine."

Some critics would be quick to point out that our
times don't lend themselves to such an easygoing philo-
sophy. They would say, "Haven't you been keeping up
with current events? How can I be anything but grim?"

To which I reply, "What are you doing under the circumstances?" Correct me if I'm wrong, but isn't the Christian life to be lived above the circumstances? A good sense of humor enlivens our discernment and guards us from taking everything that comes down the pike too seriously. By remaining lighthearted, by refusing to allow our intensity to gain mastery over our minds, we remain much more objective.

Perhaps you find yourself among those in the if-only group. You say you would laugh if only you had more money, if only you had more talent or were more beautiful, if only you could find a more fulfilling job. I challenge those excuses. Just as more money never made anyone generous and more talent never made anyone grateful, more of anything never made anyone joyful.

I like how Jane Canfield puts it:

The happiest people are rarely the richest, or the most beautiful, or even the most talented. Happy people don't depend on excitement and "fun" supplied by externals. They enjoy the fundamental, often very simple, things of life. They waste no time thinking other pastures are greener; they do not yearn for yesterday or tomorrow. They savor the moment, glad to be alive, enjoying their work, their families, the good things around them. They are adaptable; they can bend with the wind, adjust to the changes in their times, enjoy the contests of life, and feel themselves in harmony with the world. Their eyes are turned outward; they are aware, compassionate. They have the capacity to love.[1]

Without exception, people who consistently express inward joy through laughter, smiles, whistling a tune, or a soft sigh of contentment, do so in spite of—seldom because of—anything going on around them. They pursue fun rather than wait for it to knock on their door in the middle of the day. Such infectiously joyful believers have no trouble convincing people around them that Christianity is real and that Christ can transform a life. As the saying goes, joy is the flag that flies above the castle of their hearts, announcing that the King is in residence.

A LETTER OF JOY

I want to introduce you to a man who smiled in spite of hard times. There once lived a man who became a Christian as an adult and left the security and popularity of his former career as a highly credentialed religious scholar to follow Christ. Persecution became his companion throughout the remaining years of his life. Misunderstood, misrepresented, and maligned though he was, he pressed on joyfully. On top of all that, he suffered from a physical ailment so severe he called it a "thorn" in his flesh—possibly a severe eye condition that brought on blurred vision or intense migraines that attacked him on a regular basis.

By now you've probably guessed I'm referring to Saul of Tarsus, later called Paul. Though not one to dwell on his own difficulties or ailments, the apostle did take the time to record a partial list of them in his second letter to his friends in Corinth. Compared to his first-century contemporaries, he was—

. . . in far more imprisonments, beaten times without number, often in danger of death. Five times I received from the Jews thirty-nine lashes. Three times I was beaten with rods, once I was stoned, three times I was shipwrecked, a night and a day I have spent in the deep. I have been on frequent journeys, in dangers from rivers, dangers from robbers, dangers from my countrymen, dangers from the Gentiles, dangers in the city, dangers in the wilderness, dangers on the sea, dangers among false brethren; I have been in labor and hardship, through many sleepless nights, in hunger and thirst, often without food, in cold and exposure. Apart from such external things, there is the daily pressure on me of concern for all the churches.

2 CORINTHIANS 11:23–28

Although that was enough hardship for several people, Paul's journey got even more rugged as time passed. Finally he was arrested and placed under the constant guard of Roman soldiers to whom he was chained for two years. While he was allowed to remain "in his own rented quarters" (Acts 28:30), the restrictions must have been irksome to a man who had grown accustomed to traveling and to the freedom of setting his own agenda. Yet not once do we read of his losing patience and throwing a fit. On the contrary, he saw his circumstances as an opportunity to make Christ known as he made the best of his situation.

Interestingly, Paul wrote several letters during those years of house arrest, one of which was addressed to a group of Christians living in Philippi. That amazing letter is made even more remarkable by its recurring theme— joy. Think of it! Written by a man who had known excruciating hardship and pain, living in a restricted setting chained to a Roman soldier, the letter to the Philippians resounds with joy! Attitudes of joy and contentment are woven through the tapestry of these 104 verses like threads of silver. Rather than wallowing in self-pity or calling on his friends to help him escape or at least find relief from his restrictions, Paul sent a surprisingly lighthearted message. And on top of all that, time and again he urges the Philippians, and his readers, to be people of joy.

Let me show you how that same theme resurfaces.

- When Paul prayed for the Philippians, he smiled!

I thank my God in all my remembrance of you, always offering prayer with joy in my every prayer for you all. (Philippians 1:3–4)

- When he compared staying on earth to leaving and going to be with Jesus, he was joyful.

For to me, to live is Christ, and to die is gain. But if I am to live on in the flesh, this will mean fruitful labor for me; and I do not know which to choose. But I am hard-pressed from both directions, having the desire to depart and be with Christ, for that is very much better; yet to remain on in the flesh is more necessary for your sake. Convinced of this, I know that I will remain and continue with you all for your progress and joy in the faith. (Philippians 1:21–25)

- When he encouraged them to work together in harmony, his own joy intensified as he envisioned that happening.

Therefore if there is any encouragement in Christ, if there is any consolation of love, if there is any fellowship of the Spirit, if any affection and compassion, make my joy complete by being of the same mind, maintaining the same love, united in spirit, intent on one purpose. (Philippians 2:1–2)

- When he mentioned sending a friend to them, he urged them to receive the man joyfully.

But I thought it necessary to send to you Epaphroditus, my brother and fellow worker and fellow soldier, who is also your messenger and minister to my need; because he was longing for you all and was distressed because you had heard that he was sick. For indeed he was sick to the point of death, but God had mercy on him, and not on him only but also on me, so that I would not have sorrow upon sorrow. Therefore I have sent him all the more eagerly so that when you see him again you may rejoice and I may be less concerned about you. Receive him then in the Lord with all joy, and hold men like him in high regard. (Philippians 2:25–29)

- When he communicated the "core" of what he wanted them to hear from him, he was full of joy.

  Finally, my brethren, rejoice in the Lord. To write the same things again is no trouble to me, and it is a safeguard for you. (Philippians 3:1)

- When he was drawing his letter to a close, he returned to the same message of joy.

  Rejoice in the Lord always; again I will say, rejoice! (Philippians 4:4)

- Finally, when Paul called to mind their concern for his welfare, the joy about which he writes is (in my opinion) one of the most upbeat passages found in Scripture.

But I rejoiced in the Lord greatly, that now at last you have revived your concern for me; indeed, you were concerned before, but you lacked opportunity. Not that I speak from want, for I have learned to be content in whatever circumstances I am. I know how to get along with humble means, and I also know how to live in prosperity; in any and every circumstance I have learned the secret of being filled and going hungry, both of having abundance and suffering need. I can do all things through Him who strengthens me. Nevertheless, you have done well to share with me in my affliction. You yourselves also know, Philippians, that at the first preaching of the gospel, after I left Macedonia, no church shared with me in the matter of giving and receiving but you alone; for even in Thessalonica you sent a gift more than once for my needs. Not that I seek the gift itself, but I seek for the profit which increases to your account. But I have received everything in full and have an abundance; I am amply supplied, having received from Epaphroditus what you have sent, a fragrant aroma, an acceptable sacrifice, well-pleasing to God. And my

God will supply all your needs according to His riches in glory in Christ Jesus. (Philippians 4:10–19)

CHOOSING TO LIVE JOYFULLY

I strongly suspect that after the Philippians received this delightful little letter from Paul, their joy increased to an all-time high. They had received a joy transfusion from someone they dearly loved, which must have been all the more appreciated as they remembered Paul's circumstances. If he, in that irritating, stifling situation, could be so positive, so full of encouragement, so affirming, then certainly those living in freedom could be joyful, too.

Life's joy stealers are many, and you will need to get rid of them if you hope to attain the kind of happiness described by Paul's pen. If you don't, all attempts to receive (or give) a joy transfusion will be blocked. One of the ringleaders with whom you'll need to do battle sooner rather than later is that sneaky thief who slides into your thoughts and reminds you of something from the past that demoralizes you (even though it's over and done with and fully forgiven). Or that thief conjures up fears regarding something in the future (even though that frightening something may never happen). Joyful people stay riveted to the here and now, not to the then and never.

My point? God is no distant deity but a constant reality, a very present help whenever needs occur. So, live like it. And laugh like it! Paul did. While he lived, he drained every drop of joy out of every day that passed.

Before we are very far along, you'll begin to realize that joy is a choice. You'll discover that each person must choose joy if he or she hopes to live a full life. Jesus gave us His truth so that His joy might be in us. And when that happens, our joy is full (John 15:11). The tragedy is that so few choose to live joyfully.

Will you? If you will, I can make you a promise: laughter and enthusiasm will follow.

WHAT YOU'VE LEARNED

o Joy is the key to moving forward with a positive mindset and optimistic outlook for the future.

o Joy is a choice each person must make for themselves.

o No matter what you're going through, it is possible to identify blessings and things to be grateful for.

SCRIPTURES ABOUT JOY

o I thank my God in all my remembrance of you, always offering prayer with joy in my every prayer for you all. (Philippians 1:3–4)

o These things I have spoken to you so that My joy may be in you, and that your joy may be made full. (John 15:11)

o Therefore if there is any encouragement in Christ, if there is any consolation of love, if there is any fellowship of the Spirit, if any affection and compassion, make my joy complete by being of the same mind, maintaining the same love, united in spirit, intent on one purpose. (Philippians 2:1–2)

QUESTIONS FOR REFLECTION

What childlike quality do you remember being praised for when you were little? If you lost that quality as an adult, how can you revive it?

Joy can help you gain a new perspective on those harsh days when you might be struggling. What joyful moments do you reminisce about when you're going through a difficult time?

_____

_____

_____

_____

_____

_____

_____

_____

_____

What are some simple ways you can channel joy every day and share it with others?

_____

_____

_____

_____

_____

_____

_____

_____

_____

_____

CHAPTER 2

THE SECRET TO OVERCOMING LIFE'S DILEMMAS

LIFE GETS COMPLICATED.

I can't speak for you, but for me, dilemmas are a regular occurrence. Some people—at least from all outward appearances—seem to have a closed box approach to life. Stuff they encounter is either right or wrong, and they never appear to have a problem deciding which. Not for me. Somehow, I wind up in the gray area more often than not. Perhaps that's been your experience too.

If so, people like us can appreciate Charlie Brown's frequent frustrations, as portrayed in Charles Schulz's famous *Peanuts* cartoons. Like the one where Lucy is philosophizing and Charlie is listening. As usual, Lucy has the floor, delivering one of her dogmatic lectures.

"Charlie Brown," she begins, "life is a lot like a deck chair. Some place it so they can see where they're going. Others place it to see where they've been. And some so they can see where they are at the present."

Charlie sighs, "I can't even get mine unfolded!"

More than a few of us identify with Charlie. Life's dilemmas leave us unsettled and unsure. We find ourselves, like the old saying goes, between a rock and a hard place.

TYPES OF DILEMMAS

Dilemmas have the potential of being some of life's most demanding joy stealers. Being stuck between two possibilities where a case could be made for going either way . . . ah, that's a tough call. We've all been there. I think they fall into at least three categories: volitional dilemmas, emotional dilemmas, and geographical dilemmas.

VOLITIONAL DILEMMAS

A volitional dilemma occurs when we want to do two different things at the same time.

Young couples who have been married for two or three years, sometimes less, are often trying to finish their schooling, yet they're anxious to start a family. Which should they do? To start having children means extra financial pressure and an even greater struggle with time and energy drain. Yet to wait several years means they may be in their thirties, and they would much rather begin parenting earlier than that. Which do they do?

Another volitional dilemma occurs when we find ourselves unhappy in our church. The problem is exacerbated by the fact that we have been members for many years and have our closest friends there. Do we stick it out and try to help bring about needed changes, which may not be too promising and could create ill feelings? Or do we graciously declare our disagreement and leave?

EMOTIONAL DILEMMAS

Emotional dilemmas are even more intense. They occur when we entertain contrary feelings about the same event.

I remember when our younger son, Chuck, discovered that his longtime pet had a dreadful skin disease. Sasha, a beautiful white Samoyed, had been his dog for many years. To say they were close is to understate the inseparable bond between them. No matter what Chuck tried—and believe me, he tried everything—nothing helped. The dog became increasingly miserable. You have already guessed the dilemma. To provide Sasha relief meant putting her to sleep . . . an option so painful to Chuck he could scarcely discuss it.

If you think that one is difficult, how about dealing with a rebellious adult son or daughter? He or she has moved out of the home but is living a lifestyle that is both personally destructive and disappointing to you. It's obvious that some financial assistance could be put to good use. In fact, a request is made. Do you help or do you resist? Seems so objective, so simple on paper, but few dilemmas are more heartrending.

GEOGRAPHICAL DILEMMAS

Geographical dilemmas occur when we desire to be in two places at the same time. We love living where we have been for years, but moving would bring an encouraging financial advancement, not to mention the opportunity to cultivate new friendships and enjoy some much-needed changes. To leave, however, would be difficult because of the ages of the kids (two are older teenagers) and the long-standing relationships we have enjoyed at our church, in our neighborhood, and especially with our friends. We weigh both sides. Neither is ideal, yet both have their benefits—a classic geographical dilemma.

I am aware of some crossovers within these three categories, but by distinguishing them, we're able to see that each one pulls at us in unique ways. They each introduce numerous and deep feelings of strain, which can quickly drain our reservoir of joy. I might also add that being older and wiser doesn't mean we're immune to the problem. As Charlie Brown admitted, even seasoned veterans of life can find it difficult to get their deck chairs unfolded.

DEALING WITH DILEMMAS

When we arrive at such dilemmas in life and are unable to discern the right direction to go, if we hope to maintain our joy in the process, we must—repeat, *must*—allow the Lord to be our Guide, our Strength, our Wisdom . . . our All! It's so easy to read those words but so tough to follow through on them. When we do, however, it's nothing short of remarkable how peaceful and happy we can remain. When we realize the pressure is on His shoulders . . . the responsibility is on Him . . . and the ball is in His court— then an unexplainable joy envelops us. As viewed by others, it may even be considered outrageous joy.

To be sure, such an unusual method of dealing with dilemmas is rare. There aren't many folks willing to turn the reins of their lives over to God. But it works! The Lord is a Master at taking our turmoil and revealing to us the best possible way forward. This calls for a rare trait among capable people—humility.

As Peter once wrote:

> Humble yourselves under the mighty hand of God, that He may exalt you at the proper time, casting all your anxiety upon Him, because He cares for you.
>
> I PETER 5:6–7

When we do that, He trades us His joy for our anxiety. This is such a great deal, right?

As He then works things out and makes it clear to us which step to take next, we can relax, release the tension, and move forward from the dilemma.

This is extremely hard for Type A personalities. If you happen to be more intelligent than the average person, it's even more difficult. And if you're the super-responsible, I-can-handle-it individual who tends to be intense and impatient, letting go and letting God take charge will be one of life's most incredible challenges. But I urge you, do it! Force yourself to trust Another who is far more capable and intelligent and responsible than you (or a thousand like you) ever could be. And in the meantime, enjoy!

VITAL REMINDERS

Because I used to be much more driven and demanding (especially of myself), I would often search for things to read that would help me cool my jets. One excellent piece, author unknown, has contributed more to my less-intense lifestyle than the anonymous author will ever know. I hope it will bring similar benefits your way.

> If I had my life to live over again, I'd try to
> make more mistakes next time.
> I would relax, I would limber up, I would be
> sillier than I have been this trip.
> I know of very few things I would take
> seriously. I would take more trips. I
> would be crazier.
> I would climb more mountains, swim more
> rivers, and watch more sunsets.
> I would do more walking and looking.
> I would eat more ice cream and less beans.
> I would have more actual troubles, and
> fewer imaginary ones.
> You see, I'm one of those people who lives
> life prophylactically and sensibly hour

after hour, day after day. Oh, I've had
my moments, and if I had to do it over
again, I'd have more of them.
In fact, I'd try to have nothing else, just
moments, one after another, instead
of living so many years ahead each
day. I've been one of those people
who never go anywhere without a
thermometer, a hot water bottle,
a gargle, a raincoat, aspirin, and a
parachute.
If I had to do it over again, I would go
places, do things, and travel lighter
than I have.
If I had my life to live over, I would start
barefooted earlier in the spring and
stay that way later in the fall.
I would play hooky more.
I wouldn't make such good grades, except
by accident. I would ride on more
merry-go-rounds.
I'd pick more daisies.[1]

I know, I know. Just tolerating the idea of making
mistakes and playing hooky and taking the time to pick

daisies is tough for a lot of us. And admittedly some have gone too far in this direction. It's one thing to err, but when you wear out the eraser before the pencil, you're overdoing it.

Nevertheless, many need the reminder that life is more than hard work and serious decisions and ultra-intense issues. I've often been comforted with the thought that "He gives to His beloved even in his sleep" (Psalm 127:2). How easy to forget that "God is for us" (Romans 8:31) and "richly supplies us with all things to enjoy" (1 Timothy 6:17). Some of us need to read those statements every day until we really begin to believe them.

Never, ever forget that our role is twofold: not only "to believe in Him" (the delightful part) but also "to suffer for His sake" (the difficult part). That poses yet another dilemma, which would perhaps fall under a fourth category—the practical dilemma. We who love the Lord and faithfully serve Him, doing our best to live for His glory, occasionally find ourselves suffering for the cause rather than being rewarded for our walk. The dilemma: Do we run toward it or run from it?

Most people in our world today would consider anyone a fool who pursued anything but comfort and ease. But since when did the majority ever vote in favor of Christ? If this happens to be your current way of life, if suffering and difficulty have come your way because of your walk with Him, take heart. You are in good company. And some glorious day in the not-too-distant future, God will reward you for your faithfulness. You will have forgotten the pain of pressing on. And, like never before, you will laugh.

WELCOMING THE THINGS OF GOD

Among the dilemmas you will encounter, there is another one we haven't talked about yet—the dilemma of personally accepting the things of God: His leading, His tests, His reproofs, His will, His wisdom. Some people are so given to internal resistance that they regularly fail to learn the lessons that truth attempts to teach. While others spurn His ways, many glean God's message and follow His principles. As a result, they reap a harvest of joy. Those who desire to live in that joy will eagerly accept the Lord's instruction.

As a pastor, I've been amazed at the differences among Christians when it comes to acceptance of instruction. Some never seem to learn. While there are always those who are sensitive and open to spiritual things—in fact, a few can't seem to get enough—others are exposed to the same truths year after year, but those truths fail to soak in. Not until I came across three types of individuals in the sayings of Scripture did I understand why. All three have two things in common—they are people of opposition. Yet they oppose in different ways and assess dilemmas differently. Scripture labels these types of people "the simple," "the scoffer," and "the fool."

THE SIMPLE

The simple are called "naive ones" by Solomon. The Hebrew verb *patah* means "to be spacious, wide." It carries the idea of believing every word, being easily misled and enticed . . . an easy prey to deception and vacuous persuasion. The naive are susceptible to evil and wide open to any opinion. They are usually inadequate when it comes to coping with life's complexities, especially if it requires a great deal of spiritual or mental discipline.

Reading through Proverbs, I find that the simple

- are insensitive to danger or evil:
  For at the window of my house

I looked out through my lattice,
And I saw among the naive,
And discerned among the youths
A young man lacking sense,
Passing through the street near her corner;
And he takes the way to her house,
In the twilight, in the evening,
In the middle of the night and in the
    darkness.

PROVERBS 7:6–9

Suddenly he follows her,
As an ox goes to the slaughter.

PROVERBS 7:22

- fail to envision the consequences:
    "Whoever is naive, let him turn in here,"
    And to him who lacks understanding
        she says,
    "Stolen water is sweet;
    And bread eaten in secret is pleasant."
    But he does not know that the dead are
        there,
    That her guests are in the depths of Sheol.

PROVERBS 9:16–18

- are gullible and lack caution:

  The naive believes everything,

  But the sensible man considers his steps.

  PROVERBS 14:15

- fail to learn; they plunge in again and again!

  The prudent sees the evil and hides himself,

  But the naive go on, and are punished for it.

  PROVERBS 22:3

THE SCOFFER

Here is a person quite different from the simple. The scoffer "delights in his scoffing." The Hebrew term *lutz* means "to turn aside, to mock." It's the thought of rejecting with vigorous contempt, especially to show disdain or disgust for spiritual truth. Our natural response to such obstinate derision is to "whip 'em into shape," to apply a lot of intense discipline so they'll stop scoffing. More than likely, that's wasted effort. Solomon reminds us:

He who corrects a scoffer gets dishonor for
  himself.

And he who reproves a wicked man gets
  insults for himself.

> Do not reprove a scoffer, or he will hate you,
> Reprove a wise man and he will love you.
>
> PROVERBS 9:7–8

This explains why these fall under the general heading of "the opposition," not "the accepting." The scoffer won't listen to words of correction. He vigorously opposes them.

> A wise son accepts his father's discipline,
> But a scoffer does not listen to rebuke.
>
> PROVERBS 13:1

Nor will the scoffer appreciate our attempts to bring about a change.

> A scoffer does not love one who
>   reproves him,
> He will not go to the wise.
>
> PROVERBS 15:12

THE FOOL

The Hebrew root term for a fool is *khasal*, meaning "to be stupid, dull." Its Arabic counterpart means "to be sluggish, thick, coarse." Don't misunderstand. Fools have the capacity to reason; they just reason wrongly. Fools are absolutely convinced of one thing: they can get along quite well without God. Scripture reserves some of its severest rebukes for fools. But notice the presence of the desirable kind of person—the wise and prudent—in the same proverbs:

- Fools traffic in wickedness. They play with it.
  Doing wickedness is like sport to a fool,
  And so is wisdom to a man of
  understanding.

  PROVERBS 10:23

- Fools place folly on display. They flaunt it.
  Every prudent man acts with knowledge,
  But a fool displays folly.

  PROVERBS 13:16

- Fools arrogantly "let it all hang out."
  A wise man is cautious and turns away
  from evil,
  But a fool is arrogant and careless.

  PROVERBS 14:16

Strong words! But they need to be heard. They help

explain why welcoming the things of God is so urgent. Yet to be more accepting of His wise instruction may be your greatest challenge—your deepest dilemma. If so, it's time to come to terms with it. Yes, you may already have made some progress with little areas of openness in a few quiet corners of your heart, but you need more.

Few things please our Lord more than a teachable spirit. Do you possess one? This is the dilemma we must overcome as individuals. Before you're able to solve other dilemmas in your life, you must figure out where you stand and identify how you can solve those internal struggles of the heart.

OUR SELF-ASSESSMENT

Now be honest with yourself. Which type of individual represents an area of challenge for you? The simple? The scoffer? The fool? Can you call to mind a recent occasion that illustrates this fact? If you have children, can you see this same trait mirrored in one (or more) of them?

Since, according to Proverbs, no external pressure or prodding seems that effective when it comes to changing the simple, the scoffer, or the fool, the responsibility for doing so rests with the individuals themselves as they yield to the Holy Spirit and accept God's instruction.

Pause for a few minutes and ask yourself, "What are some things I can do personally to turn the tide?" Aside from hoping and praying, describe two or three action steps that will begin to move you toward the ranks of those who welcome God's wisdom. Once you've identified an action plan, choose to begin the step-by-step work right away.

There is nothing quite like a dilemma to bring us back to the bedrock of what we consider essential. Happy is the one who sets aside selfish ambition and personal preference for God's will and way.

There are many voices these days competing for your attention. Some are loud, many are persuasive, and a few are downright convincing. It can be confusing. If you listen long enough you'll be tempted to throw your faith to the winds, look out for number one, let your glands be your guide, and choose what seems best for you. Initially you'll get a rush of pleasure and satisfaction. There's no question. But ultimately you'll wind up disappointed and disillusioned.

Since I'm committed to what's best for you, I am going to challenge you to keep an eternal perspective, even though you're in the minority, surrounded by a host of success-oriented individuals urging you to ignore your conscience and grab all you can get now.

Do you want joy? Do you really want what is best? I'm betting your answer is 'yes' to both questions. Then simply consider yourself a displaced person and go God's way. His is the most reliable route to follow when life gets complicated. It will have its tough moments, but you will never regret it.

Trust me—some glorious day you will look back on the dilemma that now has you so stressed out, and you will finally get your deck chair unfolded. You will then sit down on it and laugh out loud.

WHAT YOU'VE LEARNED

o Making right decisions amid dilemmas forces us to rethink our priorities.

o Dilemmas are joy stealers. Swindoll provides an overview of the top three—volitional dilemmas, emotional dilemmas, and geographical dilemmas.

o Choosing right priorities forces us to reconsider the importance of Christ in our lives.

SCRIPTURES ABOUT DILEMMAS

o For to me, to live is Christ and to die is gain. But if I am to live on in the flesh, this will mean fruitful labor for me; and I do not know which to choose. But I am hard-pressed from both directions, having the desire to depart and be with Christ, for that is very much better; yet to remain on in the flesh is more necessary for your sake. (Philippians 1:21–24)

o Therefore humble yourselves under the mighty hand of God, that He may exalt you at the proper time, casting all your anxiety upon Him, because He cares for you. (1 Peter 5:6–7) o Convinced of this, I know that I will remain and continue with you all for your progress and joy in the faith, so that your proud confidence in me may abound in Christ Jesus through my coming to you again. (Philippians 1:25–26)

QUESTIONS FOR REFLECTION

What "unfolded deck chair" dilemmas have influenced your way of prioritizing elements of your life?

_____

_____

_____

_____

_____

_____

Can you recall your own volitional dilemma, emotional dilemma, and geographical dilemma? How have each of those dilemmas changed your life? How have you grown as an individual from each dilemma?

_____

_____

_____

_____

_____

_____

_____

_____

_____

Chuck Swindoll says, "Life is more than hard work and serious decisions and ultra-intense issues." Think about your own life. What else makes up your life? What can you do to remind yourself that those things matter?

_____

_____

_____

_____

_____

_____

_____

_____

CHAPTER 3

MAINTAINING RELATIONSHIPS WITH THE PEOPLE IN YOUR LIFE

IF I'VE LEARNED ANYTHING DURING MY JOURNEY on Planet Earth, it's that people need one another. The presence of other people is essential—caring people, helpful people, interesting people, friendly people, thoughtful people. These folks take the grind out of life. About the time we're tempted to think we can handle things all alone—**BOOM!** We run into some obstacle and need help. We discover all over again that we're not nearly as self-sufficient as we thought.

Do you express encouragement to those closest to you? Your wife or husband? How about your children? Your teacher? Your coworkers? Your neighbors? Someone who does a quality job for you?

Despite our high-tech world and efficient procedures, people remain the essential ingredient of life. When we forget that, a strange thing happens: we start treating people like inconveniences instead of assets.

How easily we get caught up in procedures! How often we lose sight of the major reason those procedures were established in the first place! Without people, there would be no need for a store. Without people, who cares how efficient a particular airline may be? Without people, a school serves no purpose, a row of houses no longer represents a neighborhood, a stadium is a cold concrete structure, and even a church building is an empty shell.

I'll say it again: "We need each other."

OUR IMPORTANT PLACE

Since none of us is an independent, self-sufficient, super-capable, all-powerful hotshot, let's quit acting like we are. Life is lonely enough without playing that silly role.

A while back I came across the following piece that addresses this very subject with remarkable insight:

> How Important Are You?
> More than you think.
> A rooster minus a hen equals no baby
> chicks.
> Kellogg minus a farmer equals no corn
> flakes.
> If the nail factory closes, what good is the
> hammer factory?

Paderewski's genius wouldn't have
amounted to much if the piano tuner
hadn't shown up.
A cracker maker will do better if there's a
cheesemaker.
The most skillful surgeon needs the
ambulance driver who delivers
the patient.
Just as Rodgers needed Hammerstein
you need someone, and someone
needs you.[1]

People are important to each other. Above all, people are important to God's plan and purpose. This truth does not diminish His authority and self-sufficiency at all. The creation of humanity on the sixth day was the crowning accomplishment of the Lord's handiwork. He infused into men and women His very image, something He didn't do for any plants or animals. Christ died for the salvation of humanity, not brute beasts, and it will be for us that He will someday return. In the meantime, God has enlisted His image-bearers to be His standard-bearers—to labor each day in this world for the benefit of each other. The major reason I'm involved in a writing ministry, broadcasting ministry, and church ministry is that people need to be reached and nurtured in the faith. This could be said of anyone serving the Lord Jesus.

Couldn't God do it all alone? Of course! After all, He's God—all-powerful and all-knowing and all-sufficient. That makes it all the more significant that He chooses to use us in His work. Even though He could operate completely alone on this earth, He seldom does. Almost without exception, He uses people in the process. His favorite plan is a combined effort: God plus people equals accomplishment.

I often recall the story of the preacher who saved up enough money to buy a few inexpensive acres of land. A small run-down, weather-beaten farmhouse sat on the acreage, a sad picture of years of neglect. The land had not been kept up either, so there were old tree stumps, rusted pieces of machinery, and all sorts of debris strewn here and there, not to mention a fence greatly in need of repair. The whole scene was a mess.

During his spare time and his vacations, the preacher rolled up his sleeves and got to work. He hauled off the junk, repaired the fence, pulled away the stumps, and replanted new trees. Then he refurbished the old house into a quaint cottage with a new roof, new windows, new stone walkway, new paint job, and finally a few colorful flower boxes. It took several years to accomplish all this, but finally, when the last job had been completed and he was washing up after applying a fresh coat of paint to the mailbox, his neighbor (who had watched all this from a distance) walked over and said, "Well, preacher—looks like you and the Lord have done a pretty fine job on your place here."

Wiping the sweat from his face, the minister replied, "Yeah, I suppose so . . . but you should have seen it when the Lord had it all to Himself."

Genesis 1 reveals that God has been in the business of ordering chaos and filling emptiness from the start. And by His grace, God invites each of us to have a hand in His great reclamation project. Yes, He could do it Himself by a miraculous flex of His will. But He has uniquely equipped each of us to play a special part in His most important project—building up those around us.

OUR UNIQUE CONTRIBUTIONS

God has not only created each one of us as unique individuals, but He also uses us in significant ways. Just stop and think. I'll bet you are where you are today because of the words or the writings or the personal influence of particular people. You could close your eyes and picture them. I love to ask people how they became who they are. When I do, they invariably speak of the influence or the encouragement of key people in their past.

I would be the first to affirm that fact. When I look back across the landscape of my life, I'm able to connect specific individuals to each crossroad and every milestone. Some of them are people the world will never know because they are relatively unknown to the general public. But to me personally? Absolutely vital. A few of them have remained my friends to this very day. Each one has helped me clear a hurdle or handle a struggle, accomplish an objective or endure a trial. I can't even imagine where I would be today if it weren't for that handful of friends and family members who have given me a heart full of joy.

Let's face it, friends and family make life a lot more fun.

For humans, social interaction is an essential part of our health. Research proves that having a strong network of support or a strong community cultivates healthy emotional and physical health. Even though each person requires a different level of human interaction, the need is still essential. Recently, a team of researchers led by Julianne Holt-Lunstad, a psychology and neuroscience professor, found loneliness and social isolation are twice as harmful as obesity to physical and mental health.[2] Think about that! Clearly, we need each other!

Relationships impact your whole life. A dilemma or hardship will hit you harder if you don't have a healthy, tight-knit group of family and friends to blunt the impact. Healthy relationships allow you to lean on people and have an established support system.

Yet coming across a person with a kindred spirit is a rare find. We may have numerous casual acquaintances and several good friends in life, but finding someone who is like-souled is a most unusual and delightful discovery. When it happens, both parties sense it. Neither must convince the other that they have a oneness of spirit. It's like being with someone who lives in your own head—and vice versa—someone who reads your motives and understands your needs without either having to be stated. No need for explanations, excuses, or defenses.

I'm thankful to God that I found that person in my wife and soulmate, Cynthia. I've had the profound blessing of finding close companionship in family and friends, too. Without them, my life would be "formless and void." So, don't ever forget the vital role you play in someone's spiritual, emotional, and even physical health . . . and the role others play in yours. This means we all have a great influence on people's lives. And with great influence comes a sobering responsibility.

WIELDING POWER WISELY

In the world of leadership, we're overrun with hard-charging, tough-minded, power-loving people who equate power with position. But people can wield power and influence in any position, as long as they maintain control over something others want.

This reminds me of a little story that illustrates positional power. A new factory owner went to a nearby restaurant for a quick lunch. The menu featured a blue plate special and made it clear—absolutely no substitutions or additions. The meal was tasty, but the man needed more butter. When he asked for a second pat of butter, the waitress refused. He was so irritated he called for the manager . . . who also refused him and walked away (much to the waitress's delight).

"Do you people know who I am?" the man asked indignantly. "I am the owner of that factory across the street!"

The waitress smiled sarcastically and whined, "Do you know who I am, sweetie? I'm the one who decides whether you get a second pat of butter."

You see? Little position, great power.

So it is in the realm of relationships. No matter how small the exchange, we have the power to impact each other—for good or ill. Our attitude will contribute to the impression we leave on others and ourselves.

A special joy binds two friends who are not reluctant to risk danger on each other's behalf. If a true friend finds you're in need, he or she will find a way to help. A true friend wouldn't ask, "How great is the risk?" The question is always, "When do you need me?" Not even the threat of death holds back a true friend.

This reminds me of the six-year-old girl who became deathly ill with a life-threatening disease. To survive, she needed a blood transfusion from someone who had previously conquered the same illness. The situation was complicated by her rare blood type. Her nine-year-old brother qualified as a donor, but everyone was hesitant to ask him since he was a young child. Finally the family agreed to have the doctor pose the question.

The attending physician tactfully asked the boy if he was willing to be brave and donate blood for his sister. Though he didn't understand much about such things, the boy agreed without hesitation. "Sure, I'll give my blood for my sister."

He lay down beside his sister and smiled at her as they

pricked his arm with the needle. Then he closed his eyes and lay silently on the bed as the pint of blood was taken.

Soon after, the physician came in to thank the little fellow. The boy, with quivering lips and tears running down his cheeks, asked, "Doctor, when do I die?" At that moment the doctor realized that the naive little boy thought that by giving his blood, he was giving up his life.

Quickly he reassured the little boy that he was not going to die, but amazed at his courage, the doctor asked, "Why were you willing to risk your life for her?"

"Because she is my sister . . . and I love her" was the boy's simple but significant reply.

Danger and risk don't threaten true friendship; they strengthen it. When we need them, they are there. I have a few in that category. Hopefully, you do too. If you don't have somebody who would lay down their lives for you . . . and you for them . . . you're missing out on a profound source of strength and joy.

FRIENDS FOR LIFE

True, intimate, life-changing friendships are becoming rare in our days of superficial companionship, social media interactions, and a long list of "contacts" in our cellphone directories. As I think about our desperate need for close, life-affirming relationships, I'm reminded of three kinds of special people God brings into our lives and how we are to respond to them.

First, there are still a few Timothys left on earth, thank goodness. In the Bible we learn that Timothy was compassionate and unselfish. He had a servant's heart and was kindred spirits with Paul, who called him his spiritual "son" (1 Corinthians 4:17; Philippians 2:22 NIV). When God sends a Timothy into our lives, He expects us to relate to him. With a Timothy, you won't have to force a friendship; it will flow. Nor will you find yourself dreading the relationship; it will be rewarding. When a Timothy comes along, that friendship will be energizing, not draining. Our response to a Timothy? Relate.

Second, there may be a modern-day Epaphroditus who comes to your assistance or your rescue. In Philippians, Epaphroditus brings money to Paul from the church in Philippi, which tells us that the people back home trusted him completely. Later, Paul writes with deep affection, referring to Epaphroditus as a "brother and fellow worker and fellow soldier . . . [and] messenger and minister to my need" (Philippians 2:25). When God sends an Epaphroditus to minister to us, He expects us to respect him. This is the type of person who reaches out when he has nothing to gain and perhaps much to lose. This is the type of person who gambles on your behalf for no other reason than love. His or her action is an act of grace. Don't question it or try to repay it or make attempts to bargain for it. Just accept it. Grace extended in love is to be accepted with gratitude. The best response to an Epaphroditus? Respect.

It's time I introduced you to the third friend. His name is Jesus Christ. Since God sent Christ to take away our sins and bring us to heaven, He expects us to receive Him. If you think a Timothy can mean a lot to you or an Epaphroditus could prove invaluable, let me assure you that neither can compare as a substitute for Jesus. In fact, it's only because of their relationship with Jesus that Timothy and Epaphroditus could be the kinds of friends they were. With nail-scarred hands, the Lord Jesus reaches out to you and waits for you to reach back in faith. I tell you without a moment's hesitation, there is no one you will ever meet, no friend you will ever make, who can do for you what Jesus can do. No one else can change your inner heart. No one else can turn your entire life around. No one else can remove not only your sins but the guilt and shame that are part of that whole ugly package. And now that the two of you have been introduced, only one response is appropriate. Only one: receive.

I began this chapter by stating that people need other people. You need me. I need you. Both of us need a few kindred spirits, people who understand us and encourage us. Both of us need friends who are willing to take risks to help us and, yes, at times, to rescue us. Friends like that make life more fun. But all of us—you, me, Timothy-people, Epaphroditus-people, all of us—need a Savior. He awaits your response. The everlasting relief He brings is enough to make hard times less daunting and good times more memorable.

WHAT YOU'VE LEARNED

o Even though we are all unique and distinct, we still need each other. We were built for human interaction and community.

o Danger and risks do not damage true friendships— they strengthen them.

o It is important to maintain and nurture your relationships by showing up for others and taking risks for others.

SCRIPTURES ABOUT RELATIONSHIPS

o Do nothing from selfishness or empty conceit, but with humility of mind regard one another as more important than yourselves; do not merely look out for your own personal interests, but also for the interest of others. (Philippians 2:3–4)

o This is My commandment, that you love one another, just as I have loved you. Greater love has no one than this, that a person will lay down his life for his friends. You are My friends if you do what I command you. No longer do I call you slaves, for the slave does not know what his master is doing; but I have called you friends, for all things that I have heard from My Father I have made known to you. (John 15:12–15)

o Two are better than one because they have a good return for their labor. For if either of them falls, the one will lift up his companion. But woe to the one who falls when there is not another to lift him up. Furthermore, if two lie down together they keep warm, but how can one be warm alone? And if one can overpower him who is alone, two can resist him. A cord of three strands is not quickly torn apart. (Ecclesiastes 4:9–12)

QUESTIONS FOR REFLECTION

Chuck talks about three people—Timothy, Epaphroditus, and Jesus Christ. Can you think of people in your life that are like Timothy and Epaphroditus? How do you respond to them? How have they impacted your life? How have such people been like Jesus to you and pointed you to Him?

_____

_____

_____

_____

_____

_____

_____

How can you improve the way you nurture your relationships with people in your community, people at work, and people you encounter on a day-to-day basis? How can you improve the way you nurture relationships with your kindred spirits?

_____

_____

_____

_____

_____

_____

_____

_____

_____

Chuck says, "When I look back across the landscape of my life, I am able to connect specific individuals to each crossroad and every milestone." Take a few minutes and reflect on the landscape of your life. Which specific individuals have impacted your crossroads and milestones? Have you maintained those relationships well? Take time to thank God for them in prayer.

_____

_____

_____

_____

_____

_____

_____

_____

CHAPTER 4

HOW TO DEFUSE DISHARMONY

IN A *PEANUTS* CARTOON, LUCY SAYS TO SNOOPY, "There are times when you really bug me, but I must admit there are also times when I feel like giving you a big hug."

Snoopy replies, "That's the way I am . . . huggable and buggable."

So it is with us and our relationships in God's family. I'm not referring to the variety of our personalities, gifts, tastes, and preferences—that's healthy. The Master made us like that. It's our mistreatment of each other, the infighting, the angry assaults, the verbal misrepresentations, the choosing of sides, the stubborn wills, the childish bickering. An objective onlooker who watches us from a distance could wonder how and why some of us call ourselves Christians.

"Well," you ask, "must we always agree?" No, absolutely not. But my question is this: Can't we be agreeable? What is it that makes us so ornery and nitpicky in our attitudes? Why so many petty fights and ugly quarrels? Why so little acceptance and tolerance? Aren't we given the direct command to "keep the unity of the Spirit in the bond of peace" (Ephesians 4:3 KJV)?

I realize that conflicts will occasionally arise in the body of Christ. On this side of eternity, it's inevitable. At times, it is essential to stand one's ground and refuse to compromise biblical principles. But more often than not the nasty infighting among us is embarrassingly trivial. And, unfortunately, the world has a field day watching us fight and quarrel over the silliest things.

CONFLICT 101

Over my decades of ministry, I've discovered four foundational principles regarding the reality of disharmony and conflict among brothers and sisters who should be getting along. A couple of these may seem like "Conflict 101," but we need to spell them out right up front before we dig deeper into this disfiguring disease on the body of Christ.

First, clashes will continue to occur. I wish I could promise you otherwise, but as long as we're on this side of Genesis 3 and depravity pollutes humanity, we can forget about a conflict-free environment. Disharmony, disunity, and decay are part of the threadbare fabric of humanity. And though our garments have been washed in the blood of the Lamb, they're still subject to the deterioration of mortality and sin. So, don't be surprised when the next dispute breaks out.

Second, not all conflicts are sinful. Not all disagreements require reconciliation. Remember, it was Jesus who said that He brings "a sword" into certain relationships (Matthew 10:34–36). Occasionally it's right to be defiant and to fight. When critical biblical lines are drawn and the issues at stake have nothing to do with personal preferences or individual personalities, surrendering to a cause that would lead to wrong is wrong. It is important to possess the intellect and maturity to identify these conflicts.

Third, sometimes hard hearts are to blame. If the disagreement between brothers and sisters could and should be resolved but isn't, then stubbornness and selfishness are likely at the core. We may be adults in age and height, but we can be awfully childish in attitude. To persist in this lack of harmony brings harm far greater than the small radius of your relationship. It can take out families, churches, and whole communities. We've all heard of feuds that have spanned generations, where the heirs of the conflict don't even remember what sparked it in the first place!

Fourth, outside parties can help with healing. Should you be the friend called to assist in the reconciliation, remember the threefold objective:

- The ultimate goal: Restoration (not punishment)
- The overall attitude: Grace (not force)
- The common ground: Christ (not logic, the church, tradition, or your will)

CRACKING THE TOUGH NUTS

When the fuse of disharmony is ignited and the bomb of conflict is about to explode, only one Person has the wisdom, knowledge, and power to defuse it. The Lord Jesus Christ is able to bring about reconciliation. The name of Jesus can soften attitudes and defuse disharmony. I've learned that the insertion of His name makes it inappropriate to maintain a fighting spirit.

That's true when the parties of the conflict are amenable, soft like clay in the potter's hands. What about when they're hard like marble? What can we do when the name of Jesus, an exhortation from Scripture, or a call to prayer seems to ricochet off a person's hard heart?

This is where a good theology of God's sovereignty comes in. That's the first key to defusing disharmony. God alone can crack the tough nuts that no amount of human cajoling could affect. He's the one who can tame the fighting spirit and turn the rebellious heart. Even the godly man skilled at reconciliation or the counselor with a track record of successful arbitration are only means God uses to accomplish His purposes.

Of course, there's nothing at all wrong with showing appreciation to the bold men and women willing to step into a conflict and lend a hand. But we must acknowledge the One who really deserves the maximum credit and give Him the greatest glory. And when we realize He's the ultimate source of every good and perfect gift (James 1:17), we'll turn to Him first—not last—when facing difficult conflicts.

More needs to be said these days about God's sovereignty over everything—from the immeasurable space between galaxies to the imperceivable space between atoms. Surely such a sovereign God can handle a stubborn heart!

God's in charge. He builds up and tears down according to His purposes. Proverbs 10:29 says, "The way of the LORD is a stronghold to the upright, but ruin to the workers of iniquity." He is so powerful that He can honor those who please Him by changing the attitudes of those who once felt enmity toward His followers: "When a man's ways are pleasing to the LORD, He makes even his enemies to be at peace with him" (Proverbs 16:7). Once everything is said and done, after our plans have been hammered out, refined, and commenced—it's ultimately His counsel that stands.

Frankly, I find the doctrine of God's sovereignty extremely comforting and enormously relieving. Not only is the burden of holding the universe together off my shoulders, so is the burden of holding my friends and family together . . . of holding my church together . . . of holding this nation and world together. Yes, God works in and through us, so we all have a part to play in defusing conflict in our relationships. But don't miss the fact that God works in and through us. Everything begins and ends with God.

A HEART IN GOD'S HANDS

Before moving on from the doctrine of God's sovereignty to other keys to defusing disharmony, let's look closely at Proverbs 21:1—

> The king's heart is like channels of water in
>   the hand of the Lord;
> He turns it wherever He wishes.

This proverb consists of what scholars call a "comparative couplet." Something ("the king's heart") is compared

to something else ("channels of water"). Most comparative couplets end with the comparison and leave it at that.
But this saying concludes with what could be called the
declarative part of the proverb . . . leaving the reader a
timeless principle, a solid theological foundation.

Observe the comparison, "The king's heart is like
channels of water in the hand of the Lord." The Hebrew
term translated "channels" refers to small irrigation
ditches that run from a main source—a reservoir—into
dry, thirsty flatlands. In other words, "Like irrigation canals carrying water is the heart of the king in
Jehovah's hand."

What's the point? The king's heart, the internal part
of him that makes decisions, breathes out and commu-
nicates attitudes and policies, edicts and laws. Yet that
heart is actually in God's hands. As a result, the king
may think he's in charge as the ultimate authority over
everything in his realm, but in reality, the entire matter
from start to finish silently and sovereignly rests with
the Lord.

Now, let me state the obvious. If God can turn a proud
king's heart like water in a channel, surely He can bend
the hardest of hearts in a strained relationship toward
peace and reconciliation!

How can anyone say such a thing, especially if

the person is an unbeliever? Well, just finish reading Solomon's saying: "He [the Lord Himself] turns it wherever He wishes." Literally, He causes it to be bent wherever He is pleased. Ultimately, God calls the shots.

If you're still struggling with the idea that God can turn the hardest heart, consider the words of King Nebuchadnezzar, one of the proudest, most powerful men of the ancient world. After experiencing devastating discipline and humiliation from the hand of God, that boastful monarch came to acknowledge the sovereignty of the Almighty:

"But at the end of that period, I, Nebuchadnezzar, raised my eyes toward heaven, and my reason returned to me, and I blessed the Most High and praised and honored Him who lives forever;

For His dominion is an everlasting
dominion,
And His kingdom endures from generation
to generation.
All the inhabitants of the earth are
accounted as nothing,
But He does according to His will in the
host of heaven

And among the inhabitants of earth;
And no one can ward off His hand
Or say to Him, 'What have You done?'"

DANIEL 4:34–35

Those are the words of a powerful king confessing how God had worked him over prior to his coming full circle.

Again, what's true of ancient kings is also true of modern bosses. Your boss. Or anyone else who thinks he's in full control. Yes, even you. God is ultimately going to have His way. You may decide to wrestle or attempt to resist, but I've got news for you: God has never met His match, and He never will. In a battle of the wills, He will always win.

I'm reminded of a well-known anecdote that demonstrates how God can instantly soften a hard heart bent on conflict. Charles H. Spurgeon, a famous Baptist minister of London, England, in the nineteenth century, had a pastor friend named Newman Hall, who had written a book titled *Come to Jesus*.

Another preacher published an article in which he ridiculed Hall. The author endured the criticism patiently for a while, but when the article grew more popular, Hall sat down and penned a letter of protest. His answer was full of retaliatory invectives that outdid anything in the article that attacked him.

Before mailing the letter, Hall took it to Spurgeon for his opinion. Spurgeon read it carefully, handed it back, and said it was excellent and that the writer of the article deserved it all. "But," he added, "it just lacks one thing." After a pause, Spurgeon continued, "Underneath your signature you ought to write the words, 'Author of *Come to Jesus.*'"

The two godly men looked at each other for a few minutes. Then Hall tore the letter to shreds.[1]

THE NEED TO FORGIVE

We've just laid the foundation of God's sovereignty over even the most stubborn heart. With that doctrine firmly in place, let's consider another key to defusing disharmony: forgiveness.

Many people view forgiveness as a weakness, but it's a superpower. It frees the soul from anger and allows grace to enter. Studies at Johns Hopkins Medicine have found that the act of forgiveness is so powerful that it can lower the risk of heart attack, improve cholesterol levels and sleep, reduce pain, lower blood pressure, reduce anxiety, lessen depression, and reduce stress. On the other hand, harboring feelings of resentment and bitterness day after day can negatively affect mental, emotional, and physical health. Karen Swartz, MD, director of the Mood Disorders Adult Consultation Clinic at Johns Hopkins, says forgiveness is not just about saying the words; rather, "it is an active process in which you make a conscious decision to let go of negative feelings whether the person deserves it or not."[2] That insightful article also mentions positive results springing from the conscious choice to exercise forgiveness: "As you release the anger, resentment and hostility, you begin to feel empathy, compassion and sometimes even affection for the person who wronged you."[3]

In short, not only does forgiveness bring emotional and physical health, it also brings spiritual health that begins to heal relationships.

Have you spent time around someone whose life is characterized by a spirit of forgiveness? It's a beautiful thing. Contrast this with the person whose spirit is eaten away by the cancer of revenge. These people are walking time bombs. Festering bitterness searches for excuses to explode . . . and it usually finds them. Often, those who suffer the brunt of another's revenge are innocent bystanders. They just happen to be in the way when the barrage of fury erupts. Clearly, a choice between forgiveness or vengeance is a major challenge we all face at one time or another.

I think Sir Francis Bacon had the right idea when he wrote, "Revenge is a kind of wild justice; which the more man's nature runs to, the more ought law to weed it out. . . . Certainly, in taking revenge, a man is but even with his enemy; but in passing over it, he is superior; for it is a prince's part to pardon."[4]

Would you like to exchange vengeance for forgiveness? Bitterness for compassion? If so, you're on the right road to defusing disharmony in your own life. There won't be a better time to expose revenge in all its ugliness. Like a tumor that will ultimately turn a healthy body into a corpse if ignored, this disease-carrying growth must be removed. The sooner, the better.

But how? Here's where God's Word comes to our rescue! First, we must do something that is painful within ourselves—we must forgive our enemy. Second, we must do something that is profitable for our "enemy"—we must show kindness.

How do you forgive your enemy?

First things first. The longer we withhold forgiveness from our enemy, the deeper revenge digs its talons into our hearts. By consciously forgiving, we remove each of those claws, one by one, and we free ourselves from its deadly grip. Yes, refusing to forgive is like being in bondage. It puts us under a cruel taskmaster that forces us to think and do things contrary to Christ's commands.

When I refuse to forgive, I rejoice at the thought of calamity striking my enemy. In the Bible, Solomon's saying declares that such an attitude "will not go unpunished." The stinging acid of resentment will eat away at my own inner peace. Furthermore, by rejoicing when our enemy falls, we somehow hold back God's anger (Proverbs 24:17–18). In some mysterious way, the Lord's taking vengeance on our behalf is connected to our releasing all of that to Him. By our refusing to forgive, revealed in our looking with delight on the offender's calamity, we get in the way of divine justice. God's Word says:

> Vengeance is Mine, and retribution,
> In due time their foot will slip;
> For the day of their calamity is near,
> And the impending things are hastening
>   upon them.
> For the Lord will vindicate His people,
> And will have compassion on His servants,
> When He sees that their strength is gone,
> And there is none remaining, bond or free.
>
> Deuteronomy 32:35–36

Because that's true, all our thoughts of taking revenge must be released. When we do, we "leave room [or give a place] for the wrath of God" (Romans 12:19). Read the following slowly and carefully:

> Never pay back evil for evil to anyone. Respect what is right in the sight of all men. If possible, so far as it depends on you, be at peace with all men. Never take your own revenge, beloved, but leave room for the wrath of God, for it is written, "VENGEANCE IS MINE, I WILL REPAY," says the LORD. (Romans 12:17–19)

So much for the first part: forgive, forgive, forgive!

THE NEED FOR TOLERANCE

Tolerance is another key to defusing disharmony. Now, I know what some of you are thinking: "Doesn't tolerating views contrary to God's Word mean endorsing sin? Doesn't tolerance lead to relativism?"

I'm not talking about condoning or commending sin or celebrating wickedness. And I don't mean applauding beliefs and actions contrary to the plain teachings of Scripture. When I talk about the Christian virtue of tolerance, I mean what Paul means in Ephesians 4, when he urges us to "walk in a manner worthy of the calling" we have in Christ, with humility, gentleness, and patience, "showing tolerance for one another in love" (Ephesians 4:1–2). Paul obviously isn't talking about tolerating sin, wickedness, immorality, and evil. That should be far from our minds (1 Corinthians 5:9–13; Revelation 2:20). Rather, "showing tolerance for one another" means showing mercy and grace toward others, letting others live their Christian lives in ways that may not be exactly how we think it should be done. It means overlooking faults, giving people space to grow, and allowing them to develop their unique abilities without fear of being judged.

Tolerance provides room for those who can't seem to measure up. It also allows needed growing space for the young and the restless. It smiles rather than frowns on the struggling. Instead of rigidly pointing to the rules and rehearsing the failures of the fallen, it stoops and reaches out, offering fresh hope and humble understanding.

Intolerance is the antithesis of all that I have just described. Unwilling to "overlook a transgression" (Proverbs 19:11), it tightens the strings on guilt, and it bombards others with a lot of "shoulds" and "musts." It frowns as it piles more shame on an already shame-filled soul. Unwilling to overlook differences, intolerance sets up one's own preferences as the standard. The heart of the intolerant has never been broken . . . not really. For many, it has become unbreakable, judgmental, without compassion—shallow and petty.

In my experience, most of this lack of tolerance is subtle. It's not usually spoken, but you can detect it in a look—a raised brow, a twisted frown, or a cold shoulder. To draw on Solomon's saying, instead of rescuing those who are "staggering to slaughter," the intolerant excuse their lack of assistance by saying, "We did not know this" (Proverbs 24:11–12).

You may have others fooled. You may even fool yourself. But the Lord knows better. He sees the attitudes of our hearts as well as the quality of our actions. And He knows when we're dishing out prejudice, partiality, and a judgmental spirit toward others.

Is more tolerance something you need? Be honest. Do you have difficulty leaving room for differing opinions on all those "gray matters" in the Christian life? Are you impatient with others who can't measure up, who aren't maturing fast enough to suit you? Could it be that you've tasted for so long the ecstasies of conquest that you've forgotten the agonies of defeat? I can think of a number of everyday ways people can show tolerance and defuse disharmony:

- The healthy can be patient with the sick and unhealthy.
- The strong have no trouble adapting to the weak.
- The fast pace themselves for the slow.
- The thin and physically fit refuse to judge those who struggle with weight.
- The productive have an understanding of the hard menial work.
- The wealthy can really imagine the pain of being poor.
- The quick minds know quite a lot of the embarrassment of being a slow learner.
- The coordinated accept the awkward.
- The pragmatic listens to the philosophical.
- The philosophical appreciates the pragmatic.
- The engineer respects and tries to learn from the artist.
- The stable and secure work on understanding the fragile and fearful.

WISDOM FOR THE WOUNDERS

Perhaps you find yourself on one side of these polarities and have trouble abiding with the other. And now you harbor pride, impatience, and prejudice against those who just don't measure up.

Don't forget the warning of Solomon, who muses over certain kinds of people who are "pure in their own eyes," whose "eyelids are raised in arrogance." Their teeth become sharp as knives. And whom do they devour? "The afflicted . . . the needy" (Proverbs 30:14). Of course! The intolerant invariably choose to devour those they consider "beneath them."

This is an excellent time to bring even the slightest intolerance that may be lurking in your life out in the open and place it before the Lord. Take a look at Psalm 139, especially the last two verses. Note David's petition:

> Search me, O God . . .
> And see if there be any hurtful way in me,
> And lead me in the everlasting way.
>
> PSALM 139:23–24

What a perfect occasion to talk with the Lord about your desire to become more tolerant, to begin "showing tolerance for one another" (Ephesians 4:2) in ways that will show grace and mercy.

Before we complete this chapter, let's consider one more saying worth our examination:

> The generous man will be prosperous,
> And he who waters will himself be watered.
>
> PROVERBS 11:25

True, the initial interpretation of Solomon's words is related to being generous with one's money, but broaden it to include being generous of spirit—broad-shouldered and big-hearted. Such an individual will not be restrictive in spirit or demanding, but "generous" of soul. The good news is that the same generosity will come back to him. Others, in turn, will be accepting and tolerant. What a marvelous picture of disarming conflict and defusing disharmony.

If more tolerance is what you need, it is imperative that you go for it. I'm thinking not only of you but of others who might suffer if you don't. Those around you will be relieved by your humility and will be encouraged to know you're striving for greater tolerance in your life. Becoming easier to live with is a virtuous pursuit.

Being tolerant doesn't mean you're weak. It's a skill good-hearted people learn to perfect so they can live with others in peace. Tolerance comes down to not putting your opinions above others even if you truly believe you're right. Creating harmony and choosing to react to life with a positive attitude displays strength by dealing with different opinions and perspectives in ways that honor others, seeking to build them up, not to tear them down.

WHAT YOU'VE LEARNED

o Not all disagreements must end with an agreement or compromise; however, disagreements shouldn't result in disgraceful, petty behavior. It is possible to disagree, not hold grudges, forgive, and move on.

o If you are helping with reconciliation, you should remember three things. The ultimate goal is restoration (not punishment), the overall attitude is grace (not force), and the common ground is Christ (not logic, the church, tradition, or your will).

o Having a growth mindset and learning the process of forgiveness and tolerance are key steps to living a harmonious life.

SCRIPTURES ABOUT DEFUSING DISHARMONY

o A man's discretion makes him slow to anger, and it is his glory to overlook a transgression. (Proverbs 19:11)

- o He who mocks the poor taunts his Maker; he who rejoices at calamity will not go unpunished. (Proverbs 17:5)
- o Do not rejoice when your enemy falls, and do not let your heart be glad when he stumbles; or the LORD will see it and be displeased, and turn His anger away from him. Do not fret because of evildoers or be envious of the wicked; for there will be no future for the evil man; the lamp of the wicked will be put out. (Proverbs 24:17–20)

QUESTIONS FOR REFLECTION

Do your best to describe the difference between tolerance and intolerance. What are the "limits" of tolerance? What are some negative effects of intolerance on relationships?

_____

_____

_____

_____

Is there someone you know who could use an arm around a shoulder, a word of encouragement, or a few hours of companionship? Perhaps this person didn't measure up to the expectations of you or others or holds to a different opinion on a controversial issue. How can you reach out and demonstrate compassion toward that person?

_____

_____

_____

_____

_____

_____

_____

_____

Since it is true that intolerance and arrogance are often related, could it be that you have forgotten those occasions when you blew it? Think about a time your intolerance was influenced by pride. How could you demonstrate compassion and react differently?

_____

_____

_____

_____

_____

_____

_____

_____

CHAPTER 5

FREEING YOURSELF FROM DRAMA AND LETTING GO OF ENVY

FOR A SEASON, MY WIFE CYNTHIA AND I WERE really into Harley-Davidson motorcycles.

I know what you're thinking. Probably the same thing a lot of other people thought—that doesn't fit the image of a pastor and his wife. But who cares? We stopped worrying about our image years ago. Should we be ashamed of ourselves? We aren't. Were we having some kind of mutual midlife crisis? We hope so. Should we have been better examples to the youth? Actually, they loved it! In fact, only a few close-minded adults didn't like our pastime. They posed critical questions like "What are you going to say to your grandkids?" Answer: "Hey, kids, wanna ride?" Or they'd whisper, "How will you explain this to 'the board'"? The board doesn't care. Some of them liked Harleys too.

During those years, we were having more fun than anybody can imagine—except fellow Harley riders. One of the best things about the whole deal is that those guys and gals down at the bike shop didn't have a clue as to who we were. We had finally found a place in our area where we could be out in public and remain absolutely anonymous.

You should have been in the showroom when I first sat on one of those big bikes. Cynthia stood a few feet away and just stared. She didn't know whether to laugh out loud or share the gospel with me! She compromised and hopped on behind after I winked at her. She couldn't resist. As soon as she leaned forward and whispered in my ear, "Honey, I could get used to this," I knew it wouldn't be long before we'd be riding on the open road without a worry in the world.

We sat there and giggled like a couple of high school sweethearts. She liked the feel of sitting close to me, and I liked the feel of her behind me and that giant engine underneath us. And that inimitable Harley roar. Man, it was great!

Suddenly, sitting on that shiny black Heritage Softail Classic with thick leather saddlebags, it was like cruising the back streets of Houston in 1953 all over again, roaring our way to a Milby High School football game. She was wearing my letterman's sweater and red-and-white saddle oxfords, and I had a flattop with a ducktail and a black leather jacket with fringe and chrome studs.

When we came back to our senses, we realized that somehow we were sorta misfits. I mean, a responsible senior pastor and radio preacher in a suit and tie with a classy, well-dressed woman who is executive vice president of

Insight for Living perched on a Harley-Davidson in a motor-cycle showroom. Everybody else was wearing T-shirts, torn jeans, boots, and black leather apparel. One guy sported a tattoo on each arm—one a snarling bulldog with a spiked collar, the other the eagle, globe, and anchor of the Marine Corps. A few people were glancing in our direction as if to say, "Get serious!" and Cynthia leaned up again and whispered, "Do you think we ought to be in here?"

"Of course, honey. Who cares? After all, I'm a Marine! What I need is a pair of black jeans and leather chaps and all you need is a tattoo, and we'll blend right in." The jeans and chaps for me, probably someday. But Cynthia with a tattoo? I doubt it.

We had quite the hilarious time with this in our family. Especially since I raised all four of our kids with only one unchangeable Swindoll rule: "You will not ever ride on or own a motorcycle!" Now the old man and his babe were roaring all around town. And our grown-up kids were trying to figure out what happened to their parents and what to say to their kids when they saw their grandparents tooling down the freeway like a couple of gray-haired teenagers. The only one of the bunch who fully understood was our youngest, Chuck. But that makes sense. He rode a Harley, too.

What was happening? What would ever possess me

to start messing around with a motorcycle, cruising some of the picturesque roads down by the ocean, or taking off with my son for a relaxed, easygoing two or three hours together? What was that all about?

It's was about forgetting all the nonsense that every single moment in life should be serious. It was about breaking the thick and rigid mold of predictability. About enjoying a completely different slice of life where I didn't have to concern myself with living up to anyone else's expectations or worry about who thought what and why. About being with one of our kids in a world totally on his turf, not mine (for a change). It was about being me, nobody else, about breaking the bondage of tunnel vision, about widening the radius of a restrictive and demanding schedule where breathing fresh air was sometimes difficult and thinking creative thoughts sometimes next to impossible.

Those rides on the Harley were about entering into a tension-free, worry-free world where I didn't have to say something profound. I didn't need to fix anyone or do anything other than feel the wind and smell the flowers and hug my wife and laugh till we were hoarse.

Bottom line: it was about freedom. That's it, plain and simple. Being free.

Free from the hustle and bustle. Free from the demands.

And free from the drama.

REIGN OF THE DRAMA KINGS AND QUEENS

The world is filled with drama kings and drama queens. And they're raising drama princes and princesses. People seem to thrive on outrage, overreaction, outbursts, and over-the-top fits. And many of this drama seems engineered to "go viral" on social media. I guess clowns need a circus.

But even when a million-plus views isn't our goal, the low-key drama we all seem to foster in our own lives can be downright toxic. It can rob us of joy and ruin our relationships. Drama isn't just harmless gossip. In most instances, drama:

- makes other people and their feelings expendable.
- fuels the fire of negative, harmful emotions.
- satisfies our desire to tell stories in which we're the epic hero or victim.

- distracts people from dealing with the real root of problems.

In my experience, people who thrive on drama in their lives tend to be as content as a butterfly fluttering from blossom to blossom. Now here, now there, back to this, over to that. I'm convinced that at its heart, this kind of lifestyle and its fleeting emotional state is driven by deep discontentment.

The addictive joy ride of constant drama drives away true, abiding joy gained by contentment and a steady, stable resistance to temptation. So, what can we do to experience a more balanced, joyous life, free from constant roller coaster drama? Discover the disciplines of contentment and resistance to temptation.

TRUE CONTENTMENT

When was the last time you met someone who was truly content and at peace with the world? Believe it or not, those people actually do exist. They usually got the wisdom to be that way by learning from the experiences of a balanced spiritual life. They discovered a sense of inner peace and contentment through their walk with God. But many folks eat their hearts out, suffering from the contagious "If Only" disease. Its germs infect every slice of life, its symptoms almost too numerous to count:

If only I had more money.

If only I could make better grades.

If only we owned a nicer home.

If only we hadn't made that bad investment.

If only I hadn't come from such a bad background.

If only I could have stayed married.

If only our pastor were a stronger preacher.

If only my child were able to walk.

If only we could have children.

If only we didn't have children.

If only the business could have succeeded.

If only my spouse hadn't died so young.

If only I would've said "no" to drugs.

If only they had given me a break.

If only I hadn't had that accident.

If only we could get back on our feet.

If only people would accept me as I am.

If only my parents hadn't divorced.

If only I had more friends.

The list is endless. Woven through the fabric of all those words is an attitude that comes from the simple choice to see the negative side of life, the choice to be unhappy about almost everything that happens. Taken far enough, it leads to the dead-end street of self-pity—one of the most distasteful and inexcusable of all attitudes—and a common root of constant drama.

Contentment, on the other hand, comes from another one of those simple choices, one that doesn't allow us or others to listen to our list of woes. We simply choose to create a different kind of list—a positive one. If we don't, people won't stay around us very long. Discontented souls soon become lonely souls.

All too often in our never-enough culture, contentment is associated with money. Both the rich and the poor must hear this. Those who want (and have) much and those who feel they need more are equally in need of this counsel. Listen carefully: contentment rarely has anything to do with one's financial status. Poor people can be content. Rich people can be discontent. The choices we make and the objectives we have are what breed contentment or discontentment. Wisdom doesn't produce greed. Greed is a cancer of the attitude, not caused by insufficient funds but poor choices. Contentment comes when we desire peace; discontentment comes when we heard its subtle whisper of "more . . . more . . . more . . . more . . ."

Look carefully at the words of 1 Timothy 6:6–10, 17–19 very carefully, as if reading them for the first time:

But godliness actually is a means of great gain, when accompanied by contentment. For we have brought nothing into the world, so we cannot take anything out of it either. If we have food and covering, with these we shall be content. But those who want to get rich fall into temptation and a snare and many foolish and harmful desires which plunge men into ruin and destruction. For the love of money is a root of all sorts of evil, and some by longing for it have wandered away from the faith, and pierced themselves with many griefs. . . .

Instruct those who are rich in this present world not to be conceited or to fix their hope on the uncertainty of riches, but on God, who richly supplies us with all things to enjoy. Instruct them to do good, to be rich in good works, to be generous and ready to share, storing up for themselves the treasure of a good foundation for the future, so that they may take hold of that which is life indeed.

RESTORING CONTENTMENT

How do we correct our perspective? How do we possess the ability to understand what's important and what isn't?

We change our attitudes. This means rejoicing in what we have, not lamenting what we don't have. And once we've changed our attitudes, we change our actions accordingly. How? I've learned three simple exercises that help me stay drama-free and content with what God has given me. Let me share these with you.

First, nourish your mind with healthy thoughts. Just as our bodies need quality food to stay strong, our minds need quality input if we hope to have attitudes and actions that bear fruit of joy and contentment. Consider Paul's words:

> Finally, brethren, whatever is true, whatever is honorable, whatever is right, whatever is pure, whatever is lovely, whatever is of good repute, if there is any excellence and if anything worthy of praise, dwell on these things.
>
> PHILIPPIANS 4:8

No matter what you're dealing with or how bad things seem to be or why God may be permitting them, deliberately letting your mind dwell on positive, uplifting thoughts will enable you not only to survive but to thrive. I frequently quote those words from Philippians 4:8 to myself. I say things like, "Okay, Chuck, it's time to let your mind dwell on better things." And then I go over the list and replace a worry with something far more honorable or pure or lovely, something worthy of praise. It never fails; the pressure I was feeling begins to fade and the peace I was missing begins to emerge.

Second, focus your attention on encouraging models. This world is chock-full of bad examples— celebrities in movies, music, or social media saying, "Be like me!" . . . "Like the things I like!" . . . "Do the things I do!" The last decade has seen the rise of online influencers whose only claim to fame is being famous online as influencers. Much of the time, these heroes of hype inspire a host of copy-cat accounts. Clearly, in the twenty-first century, we need better heroes. Consider Paul's approach:

> The things you have learned and received and heard
> and seen in me, practice these things.
>
> PHILIPPIANS 4:9

In the Philippians' case, Paul was their model. From his example, there were things to be learned, received, heard, and seen. He provided a wonderful demonstration of encouragement.

In your case and mine, it will help to focus our

attention on someone we know and/or admire—someone whose attitude and actions are worth imitating. That life, that encouraging model, will give us a boost and a quick charge when our encouragement batteries start to flash red.

Third, find "the God of Peace" in every circumstance. Even if we're smothered by discouraging thoughts, even if we're drowning in disturbing images, even if we're disappointed by the failure of mentors . . . God can see us through. As the source of peace amid the storm and confidence despite anxiety, He can navigate us through the troubled waters. As the helmsman of our hearts, He wants to see us through. Consider Paul's words, "The God of peace will be with you" (Philippians 4:9).

This is the crowning achievement of recovering from anxiety addiction. Instead of living in the grip of fear, held captive by the chains of tension and dread, when we release our preoccupation with worry, we find God's hand at work on our behalf. Our "God of peace" comes to our aid—changing people, relieving tension, altering difficult circumstances. The more you practice giving your mental burdens to the Lord, the more exciting it gets to see how God will handle the things that are impossible for you to tackle yourself. When you lean on Him, He'll never let you down.

SLAYING THE GREEN-EYED MONSTER

In his tragedy *Othello*, Shakespeare famously wrote, "O beware, my lord, of jealousy; It is the green-eyed monster which doth mock the meat it feeds on."[1] I'm not sure how the color green became synonymous with envy and jealousy, but it's stuck. Maybe you've even heard the phrase "green with envy." But that "green-eyed monster" has certainly done damage, even before Shakespeare gave it a name. Proverbs 14:30 (NIV) warns us, "A heart at peace gives life to the body, but envy rots the bones."

Envy is one of the great enemies every one of us will encounter. It keeps us from loving our neighbors, from functioning with others in a community, and from affirming people's unique worth. Envy steals contentment from the heart. Along with other vices, it robs us of peace in our relationships and replaces it with drama. The Renaissance Italian poet, Petrarch, used to say that five great enemies of peace dwell in us: "avarice, ambition, envy, anger, and pride," and "if those enemies were to be banished, we should infallibly enjoy perpetual Peace."[2]

Envy is the desire to equal another in achievement, excellence, or possessions. It comes from a desire to have what we lack rather than to give what we have. The ancients referred to it as a malignant or hostile feeling.

Augustine lists envy among "the passions [that] rage like tyrants, and throw into confusion the whole soul and life of men with storms from every quarter." He then describes such a soul as having an "eagerness to win what is not possessed. . . . Wherever he turns, avarice can confine him, self-indulgence dissipate him, ambition master him, pride puff him up, envy torture him, sloth drug him."[3]

An apt term: *torture*. This is the toll envy takes on its victims, like a man stretched across a brutal rack. Jealousy and envy work together to pull our hearts apart. Though they overlap, jealousy and envy aren't quite the same. Jealousy wants to possess what it already has; envy wants to have what another possesses. Jealousy turns into paranoid defensiveness, resulting in hoarding and controlling what we have—whether people or things. Envy is dissatisfied with what one has and wants what others have. Both of these related vices stir up drama in our lives when our words and actions begin to reflect the overflow of our tainted hearts.

WIELDING THE SWORD AGAINST ENVY

On several occasions the sayings of Scripture include warnings against being consumed by envy. We are not to envy one who is violent or to choose any of his ways (Proverbs 3:31). In fact, the cultivation of envy brings "rottenness to the bones" (Proverbs 14:30). I find it significant that the often repeated warnings have to do with our being envious of evil men and their wayward lifestyles (Proverbs 23:17; 24:1). That shouldn't surprise us. Let's face it. Sin has a built-in appeal to sensual and seasonal desires. They may be short-lived and passing (Hebrews 11:25), but they're certainly not dull and boring! I admit, it sometimes appears that sinners have all the fun!

And they seem to get away with it! Haven't you noticed? They maneuver their way through life with relative ease. They get out of trouble by lying and cheating. They can own and drive whatever, live wherever, and con whomever they wish out of whatever they want. And all this without accountability or responsibility. If something gets to be a hassle, bail out of it! If somebody gets in the way, walk over him! When we compare that self-satisfying lifestyle to the disciplines of spirituality and the restraints of righteousness, it doesn't take an advanced degree from Dartmouth to see how envy can creep in.

And while we're at it, envy isn't limited to inner tortures over the ungodly. Followers of Christ can be just as envious of their fellow Christians. It happens so quickly!

That age-old, green-eyed monster can rear its red-faced head in dozens of life's scenes:

- When we hear a more polished speaker.
- When we watch a more capable leader.
- When we visit a bigger church.
- When we read a better book.
- When we meet a better-looking man or woman.
- When we observe a more effective evangelist.
- When we see a more luxurious car.
- When we listen to a more popular singer.

The envy list has no end. Not even preachers are immune!

Envy can be even better understood—and conquered—by looking at its opposite: contentment. And contentment in one's own unique giftedness allows us to show support and affirmation of others. Look again at the list above. Does it take that much energy to admire the more polished speaker, perhaps learn from him, but accept him for what he is and ourselves for what we are? You might have qualities that the polished speaker lacks. If you both were in the same group, your individual qualities might complement each other.

Unity amid diversity . . . harmony of complementary

parts . . . that's how communities and families function successfully. That's how drama is defeated. Everyone plays a different role. You and the speaker are both different—and unique—in the eyes of God. Why not affirm and glory in the diversity of God's creation? Why not be grateful that we aren't all alike? How boring that would be!

Contentment and affirmation constitute the double-edged sword we need to wield against envy. There was once a time, perhaps when you were younger, when you felt you could do anything, but then reality always intervenes. It's possible that as you age, you "mellow out" and learn to appreciate the fact that we all have strengths and limitations . . . and that's okay. In fact, it's more than okay. It's the way God designed us all to live together, drama-free.

A realistic estimation of yourself allows you to push envy aside. The fact is, you'll never have or own or enjoy some of the things you see and hear others enjoying. So be it. There's no sense in torturing yourself. Finding contentment is much more important. Be happy for the other person whom God has blessed. Be grateful and affirming that they have realized some of their dreams—just as you have.

Now is the time to triumph over drama. How much more peaceful to be contented with our lot! How much better to "rejoice with those who rejoice"! A mark of spiritual maturity is the ability to appreciate another more gifted than we . . . to applaud another more honored than we . . . to enjoy another more blessed than we. Such a wholesome attitude of affirmation underscores our confidence in and allegiance to the sovereignty of God, who "puts down one and exalts another" (Psalm 75:7).

Removing drama from your life comes down to removing stigmas and stereotypes other people put on us, learning how to live in contentment and without comparison, ridding ourselves of envy, and focusing on what we have instead of on what we don't have.

WHAT YOU'VE LEARNED

o Comparing yourself to others and living within others' expectations will create an unhappy life which will leave you feeling like you're always missing out or you're not good enough.

o Jealousy wants to possess what it already has, and envy wants to have what another possesses.

o Contentment is not settling. Contentment means possessing self-awareness and identifying the blessings you already have.

SCRIPTURES ABOUT FREEING YOURSELF FROM DRAMA

o Better is a dish of vegetables where love is than a fattened ox served with hatred. (Proverbs 15:17)

o Better is a little with righteousness than great income with injustice. (Proverbs 16:8)

o A tranquil heart is life to the body, but passion [envy] is rottenness to the bones. (Proverbs 14:30)

QUESTIONS FOR REFLECTION

How has drama taken over a situation or season of your life? How did you react? How could a different approach and reaction change the course of your life?

_____

_____

_____

_____

_____

_____

_____

_____

Let's revisit that "if only" list. How can you apply items on this list to your own life and rephrase them as a positive statement of contentment?

_____

_____

_____

_____

_____

_____

_____

_____

Analyze your own battle with envy and your reluctance to be more content and accepting. Could envy be at the root of the drama in your life?

_____

_____

_____

_____

_____

_____

_____

_____

_____

CHAPTER 6

MAINTAINING BALANCE AND HAVING FUN AS A GROWN UP

"HOW OLD WOULD YOU BE IF YOU DIDN'T KNOW how old you were?"[1] I've always loved that question. Why? Because the answer to that question has little to do with one's physical age. It depends on an honest admission of one's outlook, attitude, and maturity.

The longer I live, the more I become convinced that our major battle in life is not with age but with maturity. All of us are involuntary victims of the former. We can't do anything about it. Jesus asked, "Who of you by worrying can add one inch to your height . . . or subtract one day from your age?" (see Matthew 6:25–31). It's a rhetorical question. In other words, don't waste your time worrying about how old you're getting. Age is a matter of fact. Maturity is a matter of choice. Our challenge is the choice of whether we're going to grow up or just grow old.

You may be thinking, "Well, Chuck, that's all well and good, but you can't teach an old dog new tricks." To which I respond with two reminders:

First: I'm not writing to "old dogs." You're a person with the capacity to think and to decide. Furthermore, if you're a Christian, you have the power of Christ within you, which means sufficient inner strength to affect incredible changes. (And if you're not a Christian, there's no time like the present to take care of that!)

Second: I'm not teaching "tricks." I'm sharing attainable and meaningful techniques that, when applied, can help you break old habits and form new ones. Admittedly the process of change may not come easy, but many have done it, and you can too. The real question is not "Am I able?" but "Am I willing?"

GROWING UP GOD'S WAY

Our becoming more mature is toward the top of the list on God's agenda for us. Repeatedly He mentions it in His Book:

- As a result, we are no longer to be children, tossed here and there by waves and carried about by every wind of doctrine, by the trickery of men, by craftiness in deceitful scheming; but speaking the truth in love, we are to grow up in all aspects into Him who is the head, even Christ. (Ephesians 4:14–15)

- Therefore, putting aside all malice and all deceit and hypocrisy and envy and all slander, like newborn babies, long for the pure milk of the word, so that by it you may grow in respect to salvation. (1 Peter 2:1–2)
- But solid food is for the mature, who because of practice have their senses trained to discern good and evil. Therefore leaving the elementary teaching about the Christ, let us press on to maturity, not laying again a foundation of repentance from dead works and of faith toward God. (Hebrews 5:14–6:1)

You and I are growing older. That's inevitable. But that doesn't necessarily mean we're growing up. How important it is that we do so! It won't happen unless we get control of our attitude, which turns us in the right direction. Did you know that one of the greatest predictors of accomplishment is your attitude? Stanford researchers peered into the brains of students to see how attitude affects achievement. Turns out, your outlook on learning matters as much as your IQ. Lang Chen, the Stanford study's lead author, said, "A good attitude opens the door to high achievement, which means you then have a better attitude, getting you into a good circle of learning."[2]

Let me urge you not to feed your mind with thoughts like "I'm too far gone to change" or "I've changed enough, I think I'll just coast to the finish line" or "Change is too scary at this stage in my life."

Nonsense! None of those things are true.

It's childish to play in the traffic of fear or let the hobgoblins of habit impede your progress. No one can win a race by continually looking back at where he or she has been. That will only demoralize, immobilize, and ultimately paralyze. God is for us. God's goal is that we advance toward maturity, all our past failures and faults and hang-ups notwithstanding.

I've seen many adults who were certain they couldn't change actually begin to change in profound ways. So, I'm no longer willing to sit back and let anyone stay riveted to yesterday, thinking, "Woe is me." Some of the most sweeping changes in my own life have occurred in my adult years. Believe me—if it can happen to me, there's an enormous amount of hope for you. Attitudes can soar even if our circumstances lag and our past record sags.

God's specialty is bringing renewal to our strength, not reminders of our weakness. Take it by faith, He is well aware of your weaknesses. He just sovereignly chooses not to stop there. They become the platform on which He does His best work. Cheer up! There is great hope.

WHAT IS MATURITY?

If maturity is all that important, we need to understand it better. The clearer it is in our minds, the easier it will be to stay focused on the goal.

Let's dive into developing a better understanding of maturity.

What is it?

To be mature is to be fully developed, complete, and "grown up." Becoming mature is a process of consistently moving toward emotional and spiritual adulthood. In that process we leave childish and adolescent habits and adopt a lifestyle in which we are fully responsible for our own decisions, motives, actions, and consequences. Once I heard someone say that maturity is developed and discerning competence as to how to live appropriately and to change rightly. In a word, it's stability. As finite beings designed to reflect the image of an infinite God, we never fully "arrive." We are always in the process of moving toward the ideal for which we were created.

I've also observed that when maturity is taking

place, good choices replace wrong ones, balance replaces extremes, and a seasoned confidence replaces uneasy feelings of insecurity. People become comfortable in their own skin . . . and they begin to find joy in life where they used to find stress and anxiety.

How is maturity expressed?

Several things come to mind when I think of how all this works its way out. Marks of maturity are emerging:

- when our concern for others outweighs our concern for ourselves.
- when we detect the presence of evil or danger before it becomes obvious.
- when we have wisdom and understanding as well as knowledge.
- when we have not only high ideals but the discipline to carry them out.
- when our emotions are tempered by responsibility and thoughtfulness.
- when our awareness of needs is matched by our compassion and action.
- when we not only understand a task but also have the fortitude to stay at it until it's done.
- when we have a willingness to change once we are convinced that correction is in order.

- when we have the desire to grow spiritually by personally reading and applying God's Word.

Writer Fred Cook once summarized maturity with these words: "Maturity is the ability to do a job whether you're supervised or not; finish a job once it's started; carry money without spending it. And last, but not least, the ability to bear an injustice without wanting to get even."[3]

Most folks I know would agree that those things describe where we would like to be personally. When we think of growing up, that's what we picture. Once we're there, who wouldn't have reason to rejoice? But the fact is, if we maintain the right attitude, we are able to rejoice amid the often-grueling process of getting there. Maturity isn't achieved overnight. It requires hard work, determination, and a growth mindset. But just because it requires work doesn't mean that work can't be enjoyable.

THE BALANCING ACT

Ever notice that teens behind the wheel for the first time can't drive to save their lives? They swerve right, then left. Lines on the road are treated like mere suggestions. Their turns are either too wide or too narrow. Their stops? Like hitting a brick wall. Their starts? Like the green flag at the Indy 500. They hesitate when they should go. They go when they should wait. Inexperienced, immature drivers are marked by imbalance. They swing from one extreme to another.

And so it is with immaturity.

The longer I live, the more I realize the ease with which we can slip into extremes and the harm that can do to our spiritual lives. I see it all around me. And sometimes, to my own embarrassment, I find it in myself. A major prayer of mine is, "Lord, keep me balanced!"

- We need a balance between work and play—too much of either is unhealthy and distasteful.
- We need a balance between time alone and time with others—too much of either takes a toll on us.
- We need a balance between independence and dependence—either one, all alone, leads to problems.
- We need a balance between kindness and firmness, between waiting and praying, resisting and cooperating, between saving and spending, between taking in and giving out, between

wanting too much and expecting too little,
between warm acceptance and keen discernment,
between grace and truth.

Let me drill down into one particularly difficult realm where balance is needed.

For many, one of the greatest bouts with imbalance is in dealing with paralyzing adversity on the one hand and overwhelming prosperity on the other. Solomon deals with the extreme of adversity this way:

If you are slack in the day of distress, your strength is limited. (Proverbs 24:10)

In times of adversity, we can either give in to idleness as we're paralyzed in fear . . . or we take the opportunity to reach down deep into our inner character and "gut it out." What an opportunity to demonstrate maturity, courage, and strength! When adversity strikes, life gets simple, doesn't it? Survival becomes our primary goal. Adversity is a test on our resiliency, our creativity. We hold up through the crisis by tapping into our reservoir of inner strength.

A far more subtle struggle is the opposite extreme, which is prosperity. This is when success smiles and things begin to come easily, when there's plenty of money, when everybody applauds, when we get all our ducks in a row and the gravy starts pouring in. When that happens, watch out! It may seem like clear sailing, but that's the time to hang tough. Why? Because in times of prosperity, things get complicated. Spiritual goals get cloudy. Integrity is on the block. Humility is put to the test. Consistency is under constant pressure. Of the two extremes—adversity or prosperity—I'm convinced that prosperity is a much greater test. It's far more deceptive.

The sage who wrote the following sayings understood this much better than we. Listen to his wise counsel, which is actually a prayer:

> Two things I asked of You,
> Do not refuse me before I die:
> Keep deception and lies far from me,
> Give me neither poverty nor riches;
> Feed me with the food that is my portion,
> That I not be full and deny You and say,
> > "Who is the LORD?"
> Or that I not be in want and steal,
> And profane the name of my God.
>
> PROVERBS 30:7–9

The man had lived enough years and had seen enough scenes to boil his petition down to two specifics:

- Keep me from deceiving and lying.
- Give me neither too little nor too much.

It's that second request that intrigues us, isn't it? That's the one he amplifies. Why does he resist having too little? There would be the temptation to steal. Whoever doubts that has never looked into the faces of his own starving children. At that moment, feeding them could easily over-rule upholding some high-and-mighty principle. Adversity can tempt us to profane the name of our God.

And why does he fear possessing too much? Ah, there's the sneaky one! It's then—when we're fat 'n' sassy—that we're tempted to yawn at spiritual things, take credit for our success, and think blasphemous thoughts like, "God? Aw, who really needs Him?" Prosperity can tempt us to presume on the grace of God.

BATTLING EXTREMES

The enemy of our souls is the expert of extremes. He never runs out of ways to push us to the limit . . . to get us so far out on one end that we start looking freaky and sounding fanatical as we cast perspective to the winds. So, we need balance.

The longer I live, the more I must fight the tendency to go to extremes, and the more I value balance.

Let's do a little honest appraisal, okay? To help keep your appraisal on a fairly reliable footing, two things will be needed:

- Your calendar or planner
- Your debit card or bank transaction history

Looking through your calendar, do you find a balance or imbalance? Too many things going on or too little time with others? And while you're looking, when was the last time you got away for an overnight . . . just to be refreshed? Is your time being kept in balance?

Next, go back over the last several months in your bank transaction history. Go ahead, take a look! Do your expenditures reflect balance or imbalance? Too much or not enough spent on yourself? Is the way you spend your money an indication of balance?

Adversity or prosperity . . . toward which extreme do you feel yourself drifting today? How are you handling the pressures? Does anyone know your struggle—I mean someone who can really pray you through these testy waters? Try not to underplay or overreact to the challenge. You would be wise to memorize Proverbs 30:7–9.

> Two things I asked of You;
> Do not refuse me before I die:
> Keep deception and lies far from me,
> Give me neither poverty nor riches;
> Feed me with the food that is my portion,
> That I not be full and deny You and say,
> > "Who is the LORD?"
> Or that I not be in want and steal,
> And profane the name of my God.

You see, for everyone, life is a balancing act. Everyone wants to know how others achieve an endless to-do list, raise a family, tend to the upkeep of a home, nurture relationships, and not lose their mind. The key is balancing the process of growing up and making sure you don't lose sight of what matters most—you should enjoy the time you have. Maturity is knowing when to pause, breathe in the fresh air, take a personal day off, and enjoy life.

COMPANIONS FOR THE JOURNEY

The people we meet along the way are instrumental to our growing up. Balancing who is present in our lives—who has input and influence in our steps toward maturity—is a big factor that helps us find joy in the journey.

So, we appreciate people. We affirm who they are. When we say thank you to someone who completes a task, we're expressing our appreciation. But when we acknowledge and express our gratitude for what others *are*—in character, in motive, in heart—we are affirming them personally.

A mark of maturity is the ability to affirm, not just appreciate. How easy to see people (especially family members and fellow workers at our place of employment) as doers of tasks, but a task-oriented mentality is incomplete. And as important as appreciation for a job well done may be, it too is incomplete. People are not human tools appointed to accomplish a set of tasks, but human beings with souls, with feelings. How essential it is to recognize and affirm the unseen, hidden qualities that make an individual a person of worth and dignity. The best leaders appreciate and affirm.

Back in the 1980s, Max De Pree was CEO of Herman Miller Inc., the furniture maker that was named one of

Fortune magazine's ten best-managed and most innovative companies. It was also chosen as one of the hundred best companies to work for in America. In his book *Leadership Is an Art*, DePree touches on the importance of understanding and acknowledging the diversity of people's inner gifts and unseen talents. What he describes in the following story illustrates well what I mean by "affirmation":

> My father is ninety-six years old. He is the founder of Herman Miller, and much of the value system and impounded energy of the company, a legacy still drawn on today, is a part of his contribution. In the furniture industry of the 1920s the machines of most factories were not run by electric motors, but by pulleys from a central drive shaft. The central drive shaft was run by the steam engine. The steam engine got its steam from the boiler. The boiler, in our case, got its fuel from the sawdust and other waste coming out of the machine room—a beautiful cycle.
>
> The millwright was the person who oversaw that cycle and on whom the entire activity of the operation depended. He was a key person.
>
> One day the millwright died.
>
> My father, being a young manager at the time, did

not particularly know what he should do when a key person died, but thought he ought to go visit the family. He went to the house and was invited to join the family in the living room. There was some awkward conversation—the kind with which many of us are familiar.

The widow asked my father if it would be all right if she read aloud some poetry. Naturally, he agreed. She went into another room, came back with a bound book, and for many minutes read selected pieces of beautiful poetry. When she finished, my father commented on how beautiful the poetry was and asked who wrote it. She replied that her husband, the millwright, was the poet.

It is now nearly sixty years since the millwright died, and my father and many of us at Herman Miller continue to wonder: Was he a poet who did millwright's work, or was he a millwright who wrote poetry?

In our effort to understand corporate life, what is it we should learn from this story? In addition to all of the ratios and goals and parameters and bottom lines, it is fundamental that leaders endorse a concept of persons. This begins with an understanding of the diversity of people's gifts and talents and skills.[4]

Now that's balance! I think we should all surround ourselves with "poet-millwrights" and "millwright-poets," learning from their unique perspectives on life, growing in directions we weren't aware of. The very presence of such people can be catalysts for growth in our lives. Affirm them in that unique space they occupy, and appreciate them for the role they have in your life.

THERMOMETERS AND THERMOSTATS

Be careful what kinds of people you have around. Remember the words of Paul, "Bad company corrupts good morals" (1 Corinthians 15:33). Just as having the right people around us can help us in our journey toward maturity with joy, having the wrong people as close companions can drag us backward and make our lives miserable.

Some people are like thermometers. They merely register what's around them. If the situation is tight and pressurized, they register tension and irritability. If it's stormy, they register worry and fear. If it's calm, quiet, and comfortable, they register relaxation and peacefulness.

Other people, however, are like thermostats. They regulate the atmosphere. They are the mature change-agents who never let the situation dictate to them. They cool potentially heated situations and set a warm tone when attitudes grow cold.

That reminds me of the comment we heard from several men who had been prisoners of war during the Vietnam War and survived the horrors of Hanoi. A number of those brave men said the same thing: "We learned after a few hours what it took to survive, and we just adapted to that." They didn't whine and complain because they had been captured. They didn't eat their hearts out because the conditions were miserable and the food was terrible. They chose to adapt.

You're probably thinking, "I wish I had that 'contentment gift.'" But it's not a gift for a select few. That kind of resolve to not let life toss our emotions around like a ragdoll is a learned skill.

Interestingly, the Greek term translated "content" does not mean, "I don't care what happens—I'll remain indifferent, numb." No, this unusual term suggests "self-sufficient." When we believe that anything is bearable, nothing is out of control. When we genuinely have that attitude, laughter comes easily, naturally.

How can these truths get lifted from the printed page and transferred to our lives? What's necessary if we hope to break the selfish syndrome and accelerate our growth toward maturity? How can you be a thermostat rather than a thermometer?

Let me leave you three steps you can take when you're feeling stuck:

First, look within . . . and release. What is it down inside you that is stunting your growth? When you poke around and find something you're hanging onto too tightly, deliberately let go. Yes, you can. Inner joy begins when you have no other gods before you but God Almighty (Exodus 20:3).

Second, look around . . . and respond. Don't wait for someone else. Act on your own, spontaneously. Is there some need you can help meet? Risk responding. Don't delay. Do it right away. Among the happiest people are those who voluntarily serve others to the glory of God. Some of the saddest are people who have ceased all contact with those in need.

Third, look up . . . and rejoice. You are the recipient of God's riches—enjoy them! Realize anew all He has done for you; then rejoice in the pleasure of getting involved with others. Enjoy the simple things in life, those things that make you smile. And praise Him for those things daily.

A comment from Jeanne Hendricks' fine volume, *Afternoon,* has helped me remember this: "Living is not a spectator sport. No one, at any price, is privileged to sit in the stands and watch the action from a distance. Being born means being a participant in the arena of life, where opposition is fierce and winning comes only to those who exert every ounce of energy."[5]

Laughter and joy are definitely connected to staying involved with people. And you should absolutely stay involved! You will never regret it. Deep, joyous relationships will help you grow up as you find yourself getting older. And the more involved you remain, the less concern you'll have with that number that goes up every time a birthday comes around.

Growing up and maturing doesn't have to loom over you like ominous, rumbling clouds blanketing the sky. Instead, the balance of lessons learned and precious memories can dot your blue skies with joyous shade and water your life with an occasional refreshing shower. Yes, you can grow up without growing old.

By the way, how old *would* you be if you didn't know how old you were?

WHAT YOU'VE LEARNED

o Age is a matter of fact. Maturity, on the other hand, is a matter of choice.

o When maturity is taking place, balance replaces extremes, and a seasoned confidence replaces uneasy feelings of insecurity. Good choices replace wrong ones.

o Contentment is a learned trait and not something people are born with.

SCRIPTURES ABOUT GROWING UP

o Not that I speak from want, for I have learned to be content in whatever circumstances I am. (Philippians 4:11)

o I know how to get along with humble means, and I also know how to live in prosperity; in any and every circumstance I have learned the secret of being filled and going hungry, both of having abundance and suffering need. (Philippians 4:12)

o I can do all things through Him who strengthens me. (Philippians 4:13)

QUESTIONS FOR REFLECTION

Can you recall key milestones in your life that symbolize maturity and reflect you growing up? What people were involved in your steps toward maturity?

_____

_____

_____

_____

_____

_____

_____

_____

Chuck teaches us how to make maturity a personal matter. Think of a time when you were being selfish. How could that situation have played out differently if you incorporated Swindoll's three steps?

_____

_____

_____

_____

_____

_____

_____

_____

What are some ways you can balance growing up and having fun in your life?

_____

_____

_____

_____

_____

_____

_____

_____

_____

CHAPTER 7

HOW TO HAVE A JOYFUL AND PROSPEROUS LIFE

JOY IS A CHOICE. IT'S A MATTER OF ATTITUDE THAT springs from a deep well of confidence in God—trusting that He's at work, that He's in full control, that He's with you no matter what has happened, is happening, and will happen. Either we fix our minds on that and determine to smile, or we wail and whine our way through life, complaining that we never got a fair shake. We are the ones who consciously determine which way we shall go. To quote the poet:

> One ship drives east and another drives
> west
> With the self-same winds that blow.
> 'Tis the set of the sails
> And not the gales,
> Which tell us the way to go.[1]

Living a joyful life doesn't depend on anything external. Regardless of how severely the winds of adversity may blow, we set our sails toward joy. It's a matter of choice, an act of our will.

A TESTIMONY OF JOY

I once witnessed a beautiful example of this. When I was a member of Dallas Seminary's Board of Regents, I had the privilege of interviewing new faculty members. On one occasion we were meeting with four of their newest faculty members, one of whom was a woman. Not just any woman, but the first woman ever invited to join the distinguished ranks of the faculty of Dallas Theological Seminary.

Dr. Lucy Mabery was her name, and several of us on the board flashed back as she told us of her pilgrimage. We had known Lucy for years.

This delightful, intelligent woman was rearing a family, teaching Bible classes, and busily engaged in a dozen other involvements while happily married to Dr. Trevor Mabery, a successful physician who was at the zenith of his career. Then her whole world caved in.

Trevor was flying back to Dallas with three other men from a Montana retreat, where they had been with Dr. James Dobson, discussing and praying about the Focus on the Family ministry. Their plane crashed, and all four of the men perished in the accident.

Shock waves stunned the city of Dallas. All four men were public figures and highly respected. Their widows were left to pick up the pieces of their own lives and begin again.

Lucy chose to do it with joy. Without a moment's warning, her beloved Trevor was gone. Grief, one of the most vicious of all the joy stealers, tore into the Mabery family like a tornado at full force. But, determined not to be bound by the cords of perpetual grief, Lucy remained positive, keen thinking, and joyful.

As we interviewed Lucy that day, her eyes sparkled with a delightful sense of humor. Her smile was contagious.

We asked what it was like to be the first woman serving on the faculty. With a smile she answered, "I have had great warmth and reception from the faculty members. Now the student body," she added, "is another story." We asked how she handled the handful of male students who didn't agree with her being in that position. She said, "Oh, I take them to lunch, and we talk about things. They soften a bit." After a brief pause, she added, "It's been a joyous experience. As a matter of fact, I was given an award from the student body recently for being the best-dressed woman faculty member!"

How can a person in Lucy's situation recover, pick up the pieces, and go on? How does anyone press on beyond grief? How do you still laugh at life? How do you put your arms around your children as a new single parent and help them embrace the future? It comes from deep within . . . because people like Lucy Mabery set their sails for joy regardless of how the wind blows.

Lucy had a quiet confidence. Not in the long life of a husband and not in the fact that external circumstances always will be placid, peaceful, and easy. No, her confidence was in God, who is at work, who is in control, and who is causing all things to result in His greater glory. When you and I focus on that, we discover we can move forward with joy—even after the horror of an airplane crash and the loss of a spouse. Everything, I repeat, is determined by how we set our sails.

JOUSTING WITH JOY STEALERS

This isn't to say there won't be joy stealers working every day to crush your spirit. Despite their best efforts at robbing you of joy, firm confidence will be the lance for knocking them off their charging steeds.

The first joy stealer is worry. The second is stress. And the third is fear. They may seem alike, but there is a distinct difference.

Worry is an inordinate anxiety about something that may or may not occur. In my lifetime of experience, I've learned that what's being worried about usually doesn't occur. Still, worry eats away at joy like slow-working acid while we wait for the outcome.

Stress is a little more acute than worry. Stress is intense strain over a situation we can't change—something out of our control. Instead of releasing it to God—who has control of all things—we churn over it. In that restless churning stage, our stress intensifies. Usually, the thing that plagues us most is not as severe as we make it out to be.

Fear, on the other hand, is different from worry and stress. It's dreadful uneasiness over the presence of danger, evil, or pain. As with the other two, however, fear usually makes things appear worse than they really are.

How do we face worry, stress, and fear? How do we do battle against these joy stealers?

I want you to ponder Paul's words in Philippians 1:6, because it's so easy to think God leads us just so far in life, then lets us go just when the battle begins to rage. Not true! Paul wrote, "For I am confident of this very thing, that He who began a good work in you will perfect it until the day of Christ Jesus" (Philippians 1:6).

I remind myself early in the morning and on several occasions during the day, "God, You are at work, and You are in control. And, Lord God, You know this is happening. You were there at the beginning, and You will bring everything that occurs to a conclusion that results in Your greater glory in the end." And then? Then, and only then, I relax! From that point on, it really doesn't matter all that much what happens. It's in God's hands.

I love the story of the man who had fretted for fifteen years over his work. He had built his business from nothing into a rather sizable operation. In fact, he had a large plant that covered several acres. With growth and success, however, came ever-increasing demands. Each new day brought a whole new list of responsibilities. Weary of the worry, the stress, and the fear, he finally decided to give it all over to God. With a smile of quiet contentment, he prayed, "Lord God, the business is Yours. All the worry, the stress, and the fears I release to You and Your sovereign will. From this day forward, Lord, You own this business." That night he went to bed earlier than he had since he started the business. Finally . . . peace.

In the middle of the night the shrill ring of the phone awoke the man. The caller, in a panicked voice, yelled, "Fire! The entire place is going up in smoke!" The man calmly dressed, got into his car, and drove to the plant. With his hands in his pockets he stood there and watched, smiling slightly. One of his employees hurried to his side and said, "What in the world are you smiling about?

How can you be so calm? Everything's on fire!" The man answered, "Yesterday afternoon I gave this business to God. I told Him it was His. If He wants to burn it up, that's His business."

Some of you read that and think, "That's insane!" No, that's one of the greatest pieces of sound theology you can embrace. Firm confidence in God means everything is in His hands. He who started something will bear the pressure of it and will bring the results exactly as He planned for His greater glory. How could a business burned to the ground bring glory to God? Well, sometimes the loss of something very significant—especially something that has a grip on us—is the only way God can get our attention and bring us back to full sanity. The happiest people I know are the ones who have learned how to hold everything loosely—those who and have handed over to God the worrisome, stress-filled, fearful details of their lives.

RELATIONAL EFFECTS OF CONFIDENCE IN GOD

The apostle Paul remained joyful because he lived with firm confidence in God's faithfulness to His plan. And in that confidence that his God had everything under control, Paul felt a warm affection toward his fellow believers. He wrote:

> For it is only right for me to feel this way about you all, because I have you in my heart, since both in my imprisonment and in the defense and confirmation of the gospel, you all are partakers of grace with me. For God is my witness, how I long for you all with the affection of Christ Jesus.
>
> PHILIPPIANS 1:7–8

The term Paul uses for "affection" is, literally, the Greek word for "bowels." In the first century it was believed that the intestines, the stomach, the liver, even the lungs, held the most tender parts of human emotions. Even today we talk about having a "pit in our stomachs" when we feel anxious, having "butterflies" when feeling excited, or feeling "punched in the gut" if we get some shocking news. This association explains why this joyful man would use "bowels" in reference to "affection." He says, in effect, "As I share with you my feelings, I open my whole inner being to you and tell you that the level of my affection is deep and tender—I feel it in my very core." Too many people live with the inaccurate impression that Paul was somewhat cold and uncaring. Quite the contrary! When he was with those he loved, Paul went to the warmest depths in conversation and affection.

John Powell's book *Why Am I Afraid to Tell You Who I Am?* contains a section worth our attention. The author presents five levels of communication, which, he says, are like concentric circles—from the most shallow and superficial level (outer circle) to the deepest, most intimate level (smallest circle at the core).

Level five, the outer circle of superficiality, Powell calls "cliché conversation." We ask things like "How's it going?" without really expecting (or sometimes even wanting) a response. We say things like "Nice weather lately," hoping we aren't talking to a meteorologist. Usually, people get the hint and stay in the realm of the cliché: "I'm fine" . . . "Yeah, I hope it doesn't rain."[2] That's cliché communication. Tragically, that's the deepest many people choose to go.

Level four is where we "report facts" about each other. Powell writes, "We remain contented to tell others what so-and-so has said or done. We offer no personal, self-revelatory commentary on these facts, but simply report them."[3] Unfortunately, this is also the realm of gossip and petty, meaningless little tales about others.

Level three leads us into the area of "ideas and judgments." Rarely do people communicate at this deeper level. They may be able, but they're usually not willing. Powell says, "As I communicate my ideas . . . I will be watching you carefully. I want to test the temperature of the water before I leap in. I want to be sure that you accept me with my ideas, judgments and decisions. If you raise your eyebrow or narrow your eyes, if you yawn or look at your watch, I will probably retreat to safer ground. I will run for the cover of silence, or change the subject of conversation."[4] Communicating at level three requires vulnerability and courage.

Level two moves into "feelings." Powell explains: "The feelings that lie under my ideas, judgments and convictions are uniquely mine. . . . It is these feelings, on this level of communication, which I must share with you, if I am to tell you who I really am."[5] I would hazard a guess that less than 10 percent of us ever communicate on that "feeling" level. To my disappointment, I have discovered that husbands and wives can live for years under the same roof without reaching this level.

Finally, level one, which Powell calls "peak communication," is the most personal, intimate form. He writes, "All deep and authentic friendships, and especially the union of those who are married, must be based on absolute openness and honesty. . . . Among close friends or between partners in marriage there will come from time to time a complete emotional and personal communion."[6]

Such depth of communication, which the apostle Paul seems to have practiced on a regular basis, brings a satisfaction—and joy—like few things on earth. And when we are free to express our feelings this deeply, we have little difficulty offering up prayers that are meaningful and specific.

The levels of authenticity impact confidence. If you're not willing to communicate with transparency and honesty, your confidence can't bring you joy and focus on the things you are thankful for. Confidence brings joy when we let God be God, trusting that He has things under control. And confidence brings joy when we keep our love within proper limits. Joy is ours to claim. In fact, no one on earth can invade and redirect our life of joy unless we permit them to do so.

A CHRISTLIKE ATTITUDE

Hudson Taylor put it well when he said, "It doesn't matter, really, how great the pressure is; it only matters where the pressure lies. See that it never comes between you and the

Lord—then, the greater the pressure, the more it presses you to His breast."[7]

The pressure on you may be intense. A half-dozen joy stealers may be waiting outside your door, ready to pounce at the first opportunity. However, nothing can rob you of your hold on grace, your claim to peace, or your confidence in God without your permission. Choose joy and never release your grip! To do this, you must cultivate the right attitude. A dictionary defines *attitude* as "a settled way of thinking or feeling about someone or something, typically one that is reflected in a person's behavior."[8]

I like this wise description of the relationship between our inner attitude and our interaction with others: "Our attitude toward the world around us depends upon what we are ourselves. If we are selfish, we will be suspicious of others. If we are of a generous nature, we will be likely to be more trustful. If we are quite honest with ourselves, we won't always be anticipating deceit in others. If we are inclined to be fair, we won't feel that we are being cheated. In a sense, looking at the people around you is like looking in a mirror. You see a reflection of yourself."[9]

In other words, how we think determines how we respond to others. Attitude is vital.

All this raises a question. What is the most Christlike attitude? Think before you answer too quickly. I'm certain many would answer love. That's understandable, for He did indeed love to the uttermost. Others might say patience. Again, not a bad choice. I find no evidence of impatience or anxious irritability as I study His life. Grace would also be a possibility. No man or woman ever modeled or exhibited the grace that Christ demonstrated right up to the moment He breathed His last. As important as those traits may be, however, they are not the ones Jesus Himself referred to when He described Himself in Scripture. I am thinking of those familiar words:

> "Come to Me, all who are weary and heavy-laden, and I will give you rest. Take My yoke upon you and learn from Me, for I am gentle and humble in heart, and YOU WILL FIND REST FOR YOUR SOULS. For My yoke is easy and My burden is light."
>
> MATTHEW 11:28–30

Did you catch the key words? "I am gentle and humble in heart." This might best be summed up in one word: *unselfish*. According to Jesus' testimony, that's the most Christlike attitude we can demonstrate. Because He was so humble—so unselfish—the last person He thought of was Himself.

You see, to live a life full of joy and true prosperity,

you must be willing to be unselfish and gracious. You must have a servant's heart. To be "humble in heart" is to be submissive to the core. It involves being more interested in serving the needs of others than in having one's own needs met. The world will tell us joy comes from getting more, and prosperity means we have way more than we could ever need. But in the economy of heaven— exemplified by Christ's attitudes and actions—we see just the opposite. We see an other-centered interest.

Someone who is truly unselfish is generous with his or her time and possessions, energy, and money. As that works its way out, it's demonstrated in various ways, such as thoughtfulness and gentleness, an unpretentious spirit, and servant-hearted leadership.

- When a husband is unselfish, he subjugates his own wants and desires to the needs of his wife and family.
- When a mother is unselfish, she isn't irked by having to give up her agenda or plans for the sake of her children.
- When an athlete is unselfish, it's the team that matters, not being named the MVP.
- When a Christian is unselfish, others mean more than self.

The Christlike attitude of unselfishness banishes pride. As Isaac Watts wrote early in the eighteenth century:

> When I survey the wondrous cross
> On which the Prince of glory died,
> My richest gain I count but loss,
> And pour contempt on all my pride.[10]

What strange-sounding words! Not because they are archaic but because everyone today is so selfish—and we are never told by our peers to be otherwise. Ours is a day of self-promotion, defending our own rights, looking out for "number one," winning by intimidation, pushing for first place, and a dozen other self-serving agendas. That one attitude does more to squelch our joy than any other. So busy defending and protecting and manipulating, we set ourselves up for a grim, intense existence—and it's not a modern problem.

Greece said, "Be wise, know yourself."

Rome said, "Be strong, discipline yourself."

Religion says, "Be good, conform yourself."

Epicureanism says, "Be sensuous, satisfy yourself."

Education says, "Be resourceful, expand yourself."

Psychology says, "Be confident, assert yourself."

Materialism says, "Be possessive, please yourself."

Ascetism say, "Be lowly, suppress yourself."

Humanism says, "Be capable, believe in yourself."

Pride says, "Be superior, promote yourself."

But Christ says, "Be unselfish, humble yourself."

When I write that last line, I find myself shaking my head and smiling. In our selfish, grab-all-you-can-get society, the concept of cultivating an unselfish, servant-hearted attitude is almost a joke to the majority. But, happily, there are a few (I hope you are one of them!) who genuinely desire to develop such an attitude. I can assure you, if you act on that desire, you will discover deep joy and true prosperity. It's the hidden secret of a happy life.

OKAY . . . BUT HOW?

You're still probably asking yourself, "How it this accomplished?" How can one truly be driven by a servant-heart and selflessness? How is it possible to pull off such an unselfish attitude when we find ourselves surrounded by quite the opposite?

In Philippians 2:3–4, Paul tells us:

Do nothing from selfishness or empty conceit, but with humility of mind regard one another as more important than yourselves; do not merely look out for your own personal interests, but also for the interests of others.

With this Scripture in mind, we must consider three things:

- First, never let selfishness or conceit be your motive. That's right—*never.*
- Second, always regard others as more important than yourself. Though this is not a natural trait, it can become a habit—and what an important one!
- Third, don't limit your attention to your own personal interests—include others. I like the quote attributed to Andrew Murray: "The humble person is not one who thinks meanly of himself; he simply does not think of himself at all."[11]

Some may try to dissuade you from what may appear to be an unbalanced, extremist position. They may tell you that anyone who adopts this sort of attitude is getting dangerously near self-flagellation and a loss of healthy self-esteem. Nonsense! The goal is that we become so interested in others and in helping them reach their highest good we become self-forgetful in the process.

Go back momentarily to the words in Philippians 2:3–4, "humility of mind." As we pursue this attitude (exalting Christ) and get involved in the same objective (being of help and encouragement to others), we set aside our differences (harmony) and lose interest in pleasing ourselves (unselfishness). Perhaps the closest we come to that is when we are forced to endure hard times together.

Martyn Lloyd-Jones, writing in England shortly after World War II, recalled the terror of the blitzkrieg bombing attacks of Hitler's Luftwaffe:

> How often during that last war were we told of the extraordinary scenes in air-raid shelters; how different people belonging to different classes, there, in the common need to shelter from the bombs and death, forgot all the differences between them and became one. This was because in the common interest they forgot the divisions and the distinctions. That is why you always tend to have a coalition government during a war; in periods of crises and common need all distinctions are forgotten, and we suddenly become united.[12]

I have seen similar scenes in California in the midst of an awful fire that sweeps across thousands of acres, until finally those flaming fingers reach into a residential section. What happens? Immediately people pull together. They pay no attention to who makes what salary, which kind of car a person drives, or how much they might receive from their neighbor by helping out. Totally disregarding any benefit they personally might derive from their acts of heroism (usually nothing) and with no thought of personal danger, they "regard one another as more important" than their own possessions or safety. In a time of crisis, when we're forced to focus only on helping others, we begin to demonstrate this Christlike attitude.

But this vital life lesson shouldn't have to be learned through a crisis. I have found that just having a large family—say, four or five kids—is enough to teach us how selfishness fouls up the works. I recall when Cynthia and I began to have children, I thought two kids would be perfect. "Alpha and Omega" . . . ideal! Along came our third . . . and not too many years later a fourth.

Now, you need to understand the kind of guy I am. I like my shoes spit-shined rather than stepped on and scuffed up. And I like my clothes hanging in the closet in an orderly and neat manner rather than drooled on and wrinkled up. And I really like milk in a glass on the table and not on the floor. I especially like a clean car with no fingerprints on the windows and no leftover school assignments spread across the floorboards.

So what did the Lord do to help broaden my horizons and assist me in seeing how selfish I am? Simple: He gave me four busy kids who stepped on shoes, wrinkled clothes, spilled milk, licked car windows, and dropped sticky candy on the carpet. You haven't lived until you've walked barefoot across the floor in the middle of the night and stomped down full force on a Barbie doll accessory or a random Lego brick. I'll tell you, you learn really quickly about your own level of selfishness.

But I can also say, with those life-lessons in unselfishness thrust upon by God's providence, I also learned a deep, profound joy . . . and the meaning of true prosperity.

You see, this is not some deep, ethereal, or theological subject we're thinking about. Being unselfish in attitude strikes at the very core of our being. It means we are willing to forgo our own comfort, our own preferences, our own schedule, our own desires . . . all for another's benefit. And that brings us back to Christ. Perhaps you never realized that it was His attitude of unselfishness that launched Him from the splendor of heaven to a humble manger in Bethlehem . . . and later to the cross at Calvary. How did He accept all that? Willingly.

I have lived over eight decades on this old earth, and I am more convinced than ever that the single most important choice a follower of Christ can make is his or her choice of attitude. Only you can determine that. Choose wisely . . . choose carefully . . . choose confidently.

Earlier I quoted from the opening lines of a poem by Ella Wheeler Wilcox. I want to close this chapter by quoting the rest of it.

> One ship drives east and another drives
>   west
> With the self-same winds that blow.
> 'Tis the set of the sails
> And not the gales,
> Which tell us the way to go
> Like the winds of the sea are the ways
>   of fate;
> As we voyage along through life,
> 'Tis the set of the soul
> That decides the goal,
> And not the calm, or the strife.[13]

My advice? Set your sails for joy! You'll never regret it.

WHAT YOU'VE LEARNED

o There are three prominent joy stealers. The first joy stealer is worry. The second is stress. And the third is fear.

o No one on earth can invade and redirect your life of joy unless you allow them to do so.

o To live in humility your goal is to become so interested in others and in helping them reach their highest good that you become self-forgetful in the process.

SCRIPTURES ABOUT JOY AND PROSPERITY

o Therefore if there is any encouragement in Christ, if there is any consolation of love, if there is any fellowship of the Spirit, if any affection and compassion, make my joy complete by being of the same mind, maintaining the same love, united in spirit, intent on one purpose. Do nothing from selfishness or empty conceit, but with humility of mind regard one another as more important than yourselves; do

not merely look out for your own personal interests, but also for the interests of others. (Philippians
2:1–4)

o For I am confident of this very thing, that He who
began a good work in you will perfect it until the
day of Christ Jesus. (Philippians 1:6)

o And now, brothers . . . let me say this one more
thing: Fix your thoughts on what is true and good
and right. Think about things that are pure and
lovely, and dwell on the fine, good things in others.
Think about all you can praise God for and be glad
about. (Philippians 4:8 TLB)

QUESTIONS FOR REFLECTION

Chuck discusses the three prominent joy stealers. Can you think of an example when each thief stole your joy (worry, stress, and fear)? What can you do to prevent repeating this from happening again?

_____

_____

_____

_____

_____

_____

_____

In your own life, how can you be humble and have a servant heart?

_____

_____

_____

_____

_____

_____

_____

_____

_____

How can joy help you live a more prosperous life? According to Scripture, what does true prosperity look like?

_____

_____

_____

_____

_____

_____

_____

_____

_____

CONCLUSION

I WILL NEVER FORGET WHEN I MET A MAN WHO told me he needed to work harder at being happier.

He said he had been raised in an ultra-serious home: "We didn't talk about our feelings . . . we worked. My father, my mother, most of my sisters and brothers bought into that way of life." He sighed. "Somehow we all had the idea that you could achieve whatever you wanted in life if you just worked hard enough and long enough." And then he came to the crux of his concern: "Funny thing . . . in my sixty-plus years I have achieved about everything I dreamed of doing and I have been awarded for it. My problem is that I don't know how to have fun and enjoy all these things hard work has brought me. I cannot remember the last time I laughed—I mean really laughed."

As he turned to walk away, I thought this throwaway line was the most revealing thing he said: "I suppose I now need to work harder at being happier."

I reached over, took him by the arm, and pulled him back close enough to put my arms around him for a solid hug. "You've worked hard for everything else in your life," I said quietly. "Why not try a new approach for joy? Trust me on this one—a happy heart is not achieved by hard work and long hours. If it were, the happiest people on earth would be the workaholics . . . and I have never met a workaholic whose sense of humor balanced out his intensity."

We talked a few more minutes, but I'm not sure I made a dent in his thinking.

A PROBLEM OF PERSPECTIVE

The problem is that human achievement results in earthly rewards, which fuels the fire for more achievement leading to greater rewards. You may ask, "Problem? What problem?" The problem is, none of that results in deep-down satisfaction, an inner peace, a soul-level contentment, lasting joy, or true prosperity. In the process of achieving more and earning more, few if any learn to laugh more. This is especially true if you're the classic Type A. Hear me out.

Something within all of us warms up to people who stroke our egos. We're motivated to do more when our efforts are noticed and rewarded. That's why they make things like impressive trophies, silver platters, bronze plaques, and gold medals. Most folks love putting those things on display. Whether it's an athletic letter on a sweater in high school or a Salesperson-of-the-Month plaque on the wall, we like the recognition. What does it do? It drives us to do more, to gain greater recognition, to achieve more valuable rewards, better pay, or bigger promotions.

Virtually every major field of endeavor has its particular award for outstanding achievement. Universities award scholarships; companies give bonuses; the film industry offers the Oscar; the television industry, the Emmy; the music industry, the Grammy; and the writing industry, the Pulitzer Prize. The athletic world has an entire spectrum of honors. Whether garnering individual awards for exceptional achievement or team trophies for championship play, winning players are applauded, and record-setting coaches are affirmed (and envied).

Many years ago, I was sitting in the Great Western Forum watching the Los Angeles Lakers. I looked up toward the ceiling and saw all those NBA championship banners hanging high. I glanced toward one wall bright with spotlights and read the names on jerseys that have been retired: Chamberlain, Abdul-Jabbar, Johnson, and Bryant. What an honor to have one's name placed on public display for all the world to see! It's society's way of saying, "You are great!"

Now, there's nothing wrong with that as long as we

remember it's an earthly system exalting earthly people who are rewarded for earthly accomplishments. But how easy it is to forget that not one of those accomplishments gives a person what he or she may lack deep within! That's why they can't bring lasting satisfaction. And much more importantly, none of them earns God's favor.

Those who hang tough, refusing to give up no matter how difficult or demanding or disappointing the challenges may be, are the ones who stand the best chance of winning. They are also the ones who find the greatest satisfaction and delight in their years on earth. Henry David Thoreau said it best: "If one advances confidently in the direction of his dreams, and endeavors to live the life which he has imagined, he will meet with a success unexpected in common hours."[1]

That may sound like the ending to a fairy tale, almost as if some Disney character were telling us to wish upon a star while standing near the castle in Fantasyland, but it's not that at all. I see in Thoreau's statement a long and untiring determination in the same direction. Not a get-rich-quick scheme or some overnight success plan, but a confident advancement in the right direction over the long haul. Dreams are important, no question; yet they must be mixed with the patient discipline of staying at the tough tasks, regardless.

TIMELY AND TIMELESS REMINDERS

Don't forget the whole reason for this book. Life is ten percent what happens to you and ninety percent how you react. You have a say in your happiness. You control your attitude. You steer your success. And all of this as we trust in God, look to Christ, and depend on the Spirit. In light of everything we've explored in this book, remember five crucial principles:

1. The plan is progress . . . not perfection!

Part of the reason "hanging tough" is tough is the imperfection that continues to mark our lives. Frequent reminders of our humanity still rear their ugly heads. That's true of ourselves, and it's true of others. We, ourselves, are imperfect, living in an imperfect world, surrounded by imperfect people, who continue to model imperfections on a daily basis. Happy is the person who keeps that in mind. You will find that life is not nearly as galling if you remember that the goal is to press on in spite of the lack of perfection.

Perfectionists have a whale of a battle with this. They want life to be lived flawlessly by everyone. That's why I have said for years that perfectionists are people who take pains—and give them to others. Nevertheless, progress is the main agenda of life. If you can see changes in your own life as compared to, say, a year ago or more, take heart! You're on the right road.

2. The past is over . . . forget it!

Some of the unhappiest people I have ever known are living their lives looking over their shoulders. What a waste! Nothing back there can be changed.

What's in the past? Only two things: great attainments and accomplishments that could either make us proud by reliving them or indifferent by resting on them . . . or failures and defeats that cannot help but rouse feelings of guilt and shame. Why in the world would anyone want to return to that quagmire? I have never been able to figure that one out. By recalling those inglorious, ineffective events of yesterday, our energy is sapped for facing the demands of today. Rehearsing those wrongs, now forgiven in grace, derails and demoralizes us. There are few joy stealers more insidious than past memories that haunt our minds. Paul says to forget the past! Good advice to all who hope to hang tough.

3. The future holds out hope . . . reach for it!

The analogy is clear. In this race called life, we are to face forward, anticipating what lies ahead, ever stretching and reaching, making life a passionate, adventurous quest. Life was never meant to be a passive coexistence with enemy forces as we await our heavenly home. But it's easy to do that, especially when we arrive at a certain age, to sort of shift into neutral and take whatever comes our way.

Let me pause here in midstream and ask you three direct questions:

- Have you left the past—I mean fully moved on beyond it?
- Are you making progress—some kind of deliberate progress with your life?
- Do you passionately pursue some dream—some specific goal?

Robert Ballard suddenly flashes into my mind. Does that name mean anything to you?

Robert Ballard was a man with a quest. He wanted to find the Titanic. And on September 1, 1985, he discovered the sunken ship in the North Atlantic, more than 350 miles off the coast of Newfoundland. I get chills when I read his description of the first time he sent down that bright probe light and saw that sight more than two miles below the surface of those cold waters:

My first direct view of Titanic lasted less than two minutes, but the stark sight of her immense black hull towering above the ocean floor will remain forever ingrained in my memory. My lifelong dream was to find this great ship and during the past thirteen years the quest for her has dominated my life.[2]

What is your particular quest? For what are you reaching? There is something wonderfully exciting about reaching into the future with excited anticipation, and those who pursue new adventures through life stay younger, think better, and have more fun!

4. The secret is a determined attitude . . . maintain it!

Earlier, I talked about Paul specifically having the right attitude. Attitude is such a vital ingredient in the life of anyone who plans to hang tough. The right attitude is important for those who are on the road to maturity . . . who are growing and are ready for the next lesson to be learned.

You've probably noticed (I haven't been subtle) that this book is all about cultivating the right attitudes: finding joy even in the midst of troubles, overcoming life's dilemmas, nurturing contentment, maintaining

right relationships, defusing disharmony, freeing yourself from drama, maintaining balance, and enjoying a
truly happy and prosperous life. The right attitude in
all these things is ultimately determined by what goes
on in your head and in your heart . . . not ultimately by
what's happened to you in the past, what's happening in
the present, or what may happen in the future. Never
forget that.

5. The need is keeping a high standard . . . together.

Those who hang tough do better when doing so with
others. That is especially true in times of severe crisis. As
Benjamin Franklin said at the signing of the Declaration
of Independence, "We must all hang together, or assuredly
we shall all hang separately."[3] And while pulling together,
we need to keep a high standard. As the apostle wrote to
his Philippian friends, "Let us keep living by that same
standard" (Philippians 3:16).

Agreeing on the same basics while encouraging each
other to hang in there day after day is one of the many
benefits of locking arms in close friendship with a group
of Christians. The group not only holds us accountable
but also reminds us we are not alone. I have found that
I don't get as weary when I pull up close alongside a few

like-minded brothers and take the time to cultivate meaningful relationships. It's practical and biblical:

> And let us not lose heart in doing good, for in due time we shall reap if we do not grow weary. (Galatians 6:9)
>
> Therefore, my beloved brethren, be steadfast, immovable, always abounding in the work of the Lord, knowing that your toil is not in vain in the Lord. (1 Corinthians 15:58)

I hope our time together has provided you with wisdom and a trustworthy resource for finding joy, overcoming life's dilemmas, maintaining relationships, defusing disharmony, ridding yourself of drama, discovering balance and maturity, and living a happy, truly prosperous life.

Of course, each of us experiences life in a different way. Some of you will sort of slide through life with normal scratches and bruises. Others will experience unimaginable trauma or unthinkable loss. Many will limp along with chronic ailments . . . or be dragged along by calamities. Some will face trials and extreme hardships, others with mental, emotional, and psychological pain.

No one can control what happens to them. Such things are "above our pay grade." But we can control how we choose to deal with what happens to us.

CONCLUSION

You see, it's all about how you respond to what life presents. If you maintain a positive attitude, choose to put one step in front of the other with a joyful heart, and get back up when you take a tumble . . . you'll have lived a wonderful life.

Because, more than ever, I am convinced that life is 10 percent what happens to you and 90 percent how you react.

PRAYING THE SCRIPTURES

CHAPTER 1: FINDING JOY

In Your presence is fullness of joy; in Your right hand there are pleasures forever. **Psalm 16:11**

When my anxious thoughts multiply within me, Your consolations delight my soul. **Psalm 94:19**

O come, let us sing for joy to the LORD, let us shout joyfully to the rock of our salvation. Let us come before His presence with thanksgiving, let us shout joyfully to Him with psalms. **Psalm 95:1–2**

This is the day which the LORD has made; let us rejoice and be glad in it. **Psalm 118:24**

A joyful heart is good medicine, but a broken spirit dries up the bones. **Proverbs 17:22**

I will rejoice greatly in the LORD, my soul will exult in my God. **Isaiah 61:10**

Though the fig tree should not blossom, and there be no fruit on the vines, though the yield of the olive should fail, and the fields produce no food, though the flock should be cut off from the fold and there be no cattle in the stalls, yet I will exult in the LORD, I will rejoice in the God of my salvation. **Habakkuk 3:17**

Rejoice always; pray without ceasing; in everything give thanks; for this is God's will for you in Christ Jesus. **1 Thessalonians 5:16–18**

Consider it all joy, my brethren, when you encounter various trials, knowing that the testing of your faith produces endurance. And let endurance have its perfect result, so that you may be perfect and complete, lacking in nothing. **James 1:2–4**

But to the degree that you share the sufferings of Christ, keep on rejoicing, so that also at the revelation of His glory you may rejoice with exultation. **1 Peter 4:13**

CHAPTER 2: THE SECRET TO OVERCOMING LIFE'S DILEMMAS

Make me know Your ways, O LORD; teach me Your paths. Lead me in Your truth and teach me, for You are the God of my salvation; for You I wait all the day. **Psalm 25:4–5**

I will instruct you and teach you in the way which you should go; I will counsel you with My eye upon you. **Psalm 32:8**

Cast your burden upon the LORD and He will sustain you; He will never allow the righteous to be shaken. **Psalm 55:22**

Teach me Your way, O LORD; I will walk in Your truth; unite my heart to fear Your name. **Psalm 86:11**

How can a young man keep his way pure? By keeping it according to Your word. **Psalm 119:9**

Trust in the LORD with all your heart and do not lean on your own understanding. In all your ways acknowledge Him, and He will make your paths straight. **Proverbs 3:5–6**

The mind of man plans his way, but the LORD directs his steps. **Proverbs 16:9**

Do not fear, for I am with you; do not anxiously look about you, for I am your God. I will strengthen you, surely I will help you, surely I will uphold you with My righteous right hand. **Isaiah 41:10**

But if any of you lacks wisdom, let him ask of God, who gives to all generously and without reproach, and it will be given to him. **James 1:5**

Now to Him who is able to keep you from stumbling, and to make you stand in the presence of His glory blameless with great joy, to the only God our Savior, through Jesus Christ our Lord, be glory, majesty, dominion and authority, before all time and now and forever. Amen. **Jude 1:24–25**

CHAPTER 3: MAINTAINING RELATIONSHIPS WITH THE PEOPLE IN YOUR LIFE

Then the LORD God said, "It is not good for the man to be alone; I will make him a helper suitable for him." **Genesis 2:18**

A friend loves at all times, and a brother is born for adversity. **Proverbs 17:17**

Iron sharpens iron, so one man sharpens another. **Proverbs 27:17**

If I then, the Lord and the Teacher, washed your feet, you also ought to wash one another's feet. **John 13:14**

For through the grace given to me I say to everyone among you not to think more highly of himself than he ought to think; but to think so as to have sound judgment, as God has allotted to each a measure of faith. For just as we have many members in one body and all the members do not have the same function, so we, who are many, are one body in Christ, and individually members of one another. **Romans 12:3–5**

Be devoted to one another in brotherly love; give preference to one another in honor. **Romans 12:10**

For you were called to freedom, brethren; only do not turn your freedom into an opportunity for the flesh, but through love serve one another." **Galatians 5:13**

Therefore, encourage one another and build up one another, just as you also are doing. **1 Thessalonians 5:11**

And let us consider how to stimulate one another to love and good deeds, not forsaking our own assembling together, as is the habit of some, but encouraging one another; and all the more as you see the day drawing near." **Hebrews 10:24–25**

As each one has received a special gift, employ it in serving one another as good stewards of the manifold grace of God. **1 Peter 4:10**

CHAPTER 4: HOW TO DEFUSE DISHARMONY

But I say to you, love your enemies and pray for those who persecute you. **Matthew 5:44**

So then we pursue the things which make for peace and the building up of one another. **Romans 14:19**

Now may the God who gives perseverance and encouragement grant you to be of the same mind with one another according to Christ Jesus, so that with one accord you may with one voice glorify the God and Father of our Lord Jesus Christ. Therefore, accept one another, just as Christ also accepted us to the glory of God. **Romans 15:5–7**

For just as the body is one and yet has many members, and all the members of the body, though they are many, are one body, so also is Christ. For by one Spirit we were all baptized into one body, whether Jews or Greeks, whether slaves or free, and we were all made to drink of one Spirit. **1 Corinthians 12:12–13**

Finally, brethren, rejoice, be made complete, be comforted, be like-minded, live in peace; and the God of love and peace will be with you. **2 Corinthians 13:11**

Let all bitterness and wrath and anger and clamor and slander be put away from you, along with all malice. Be kind to one another, tender-hearted, forgiving each other, just as God in Christ also has forgiven you. **Ephesians 4:31–32**

So, as those who have been chosen of God, holy and beloved, put on a heart of compassion, kindness, humility, gentleness and patience; bearing with one another, and forgiving each other, whoever has a complaint against anyone; just as the Lord forgave you, so also should you. Beyond all these things put on love, which is the perfect bond of unity. **Colossians 3:12–14**

Pursue peace with all men, and the sanctification without which no one will see the Lord. See to it that no one comes short of the grace of God; that no root of bitterness springing up causes trouble, and by it many be defiled. **Hebrews 12:14–15**

To sum up, all of you be harmonious, sympathetic, brotherly, kindhearted, and humble in spirit; not returning evil for evil or insult for insult, but giving a blessing instead; for you were called for the very purpose that you might inherit a blessing. **1 Peter 3:8–9**

"No one has seen God at any time; if we love one another, God abides in us, and His love is perfected in us. **1 John 4:12**

CHAPTER 5: FREEING YOURSELF FROM DRAMA AND LETTING GO OF ENVY

He who loves money will not be satisfied with money, nor he who loves abundance with its income. This too is vanity. **Ecclesiastes 5:10**

Do not store up for yourselves treasures on earth, where moth and rust destroy, and where thieves break in and steal. But store up for yourselves treasures in heaven, where neither moth nor rust destroys, and where thieves do not break in or steal; for where your treasure is, there your heart will be also. **Matthew 6:19–21**

For what does it profit a man to gain the whole world, and forfeit his soul? **Mark 8:36**

Then He said to them, "Beware, and be on your guard against every form of greed; for not even when one has an abundance does his life consist of his possessions." **Luke 12:15**

For am I now seeking the favor of men, or of God? Or am I striving to please men? If I were still trying to please men, I would not be a bond-servant of Christ. **Galatians 1:10**

For the whole Law is fulfilled in one word, in the statement, "You shall love your neighbor as yourself." But if you bite and devour one another, take care that you are not consumed by one another. But I say, walk by the Spirit, and you will not carry out the desire of the flesh. **Galatians 5:14–16**

Now those who belong to Christ Jesus have crucified the flesh with its passions and desires. If we live by the Spirit, let us also walk by Spirit. Let us not become boastful, challenging one another, envying one another. **Galatians 5:24–26**

Make sure that your character is free from the love of money, being content with what you have; for He Himself has said, "I will never desert you, nor will I ever forsake you." **Hebrews 13:5**

What is the source of quarrels and conflicts among you? Is not the source your pleasures that wage war in your members? You lust and do not have; so you commit murder. You are envious and cannot obtain; so you fight and quarrel. You do not have because you do not ask. You ask and do not receive, because you ask with the wrong motives, so that you may spend it on your pleasures. You adulteresses, do you not know that friendship with the world is hostility toward God? Therefore whoever wants to be a friend of the world makes himself an enemy of God. **James 4:1–4**

Do not love the world nor the things in the world. If anyone loves the world, the love of the Father is not in him. For all that is in the world, the lust of the flesh and the lust of the eyes and the boastful pride of life, is not from the Father, but is from the world. The world is passing away, and also its lusts; but the one who does the will of God lives forever. **1 John 2:15–17**

CHAPTER 6: MAINTAINING BALANCE AND HAVING FUN AS A GROWN UP

Do you not know that those who run in a race all run, but only one receives the prize? Run in such a way that you may win. Everyone who competes in the games exercises self-control in all things. They then do it to obtain a perishable wreath, but we an imperishable. Therefore I run in such a way, as not without aim; I box in such a way, as not beating the air; but I discipline my body and make it my slave, so that, after I have preached to others, I myself will not be disqualified. **1 Corinthians 9:24–27**

Brethren, do not be children in your thinking; yet in evil be infants, but in your thinking be mature. **1 Corinthians 14:20**

For this reason also, since the day we heard of it, we have not ceased to pray for you and to ask that you may be filled with the knowledge of His will in all spiritual wisdom and understanding, so that you will walk in a manner worthy of the Lord, to please Him in all respects, bearing fruit in every good work and increasing in the knowledge of God. **Colossians 1:9–10**

On the other hand, discipline yourself for the purpose of godliness; for bodily discipline is only of little profit, but godliness is profitable for all things, since it holds promise for the present life and also for the life to come. **1 Timothy 4:7–8**

Let no one look down on your youthfulness, but rather in speech, conduct, love, faith and purity, show yourself an example of those who believe. **1 Timothy 4:12**

Now flee from youthful lusts and pursue righteousness, faith, love and peace, with those who call on the Lord from a pure heart. **2 Timothy 2:22**

You, however, continue in the things you have learned and become convinced of, knowing from whom you have learned them, and that from childhood you have known the sacred writings which are able to give you the wisdom that leads to salvation through faith which is in Christ Jesus. **2 Timothy 3:14–15**

Grace and peace be multiplied to you in the knowledge of God and of Jesus our Lord; seeing that His divine power has granted to us everything pertaining to life and godliness, through the true knowledge of Him who called us by His own glory and excellence. **2 Peter 1:2–3**

Now for this very reason also, applying all diligence, in your faith supply moral excellence, and in your moral excellence, knowledge, and in your knowledge, self-control, and in your self-control, perseverance, and in your perseverance, godliness, and in your godliness, brotherly kindness, and in your brotherly kindness, love. For if these qualities are yours and are increasing, they render you neither useless nor unfruitful in the true knowledge of our Lord Jesus Christ. **2 Peter 1:5–8**

You therefore, beloved, knowing this beforehand, be on your guard so that you are not carried away by the error of unprincipled men and fall from your own steadfastness, but grow in the grace and knowledge of our Lord and Savior Jesus Christ. To Him be the glory, both now and to the day of eternity. Amen. **2 Peter 3:17–18**

CHAPTER 7: HOW TO HAVE A JOYFUL AND PROSPEROUS LIFE

But let all who take refuge in You be glad, let them ever sing for joy; and may You shelter them, that those who love Your name may exult in You. **Psalm 5:11**

I have set the LORD continually before me; because He is at my right hand, I will not be shaken. Therefore my heart is glad and my glory rejoices; my flesh also will dwell securely. **Psalm 16:8–9**

The LORD is my light and my salvation; whom shall I fear? The LORD is the defense of my life; whom shall I dread? **Psalm 27:1**

But as for me, I shall sing of Your strength; yes, I shall joyfully sing of Your lovingkindness in the morning, for You have been my stronghold and a refuge in the day of my distress. **Psalm 59:16**

The fear of man brings a snare, but he who trusts in the LORD will be exalted. **Proverbs 29:25**

The steadfast of mind You will keep in perfect peace, because he trusts in You. **Isaiah 26:3**

"For I know the plans that I have for you," declares the LORD, "plans for welfare and not for calamity to give you a future and a hope. **Jeremiah 29:11**

Peace I leave you, My peace I give to you; not as the world gives do I give to you. Do not let your heart be troubled, nor let it be fearful. **John 14:27**

These things I have spoken to you, so that in Me you may have peace. In the world you have tribulation, but take courage; I have overcome the world. **John 16:33**

In this you greatly rejoice, even though now for a little while, if necessary, you have been distressed by various trials, so that the proof of your faith, being more precious than gold which is perishable, even though tested by fire, may be found to result in praise and glory and honor at the revelation of Jesus Christ. **1 Peter 1:6–7**

Chapter 1: Finding Joy

1. Jane Canfield, in *Quote/Unquote*, comp. Lloyd Cory (Wheaton, IL: Victor, 1977), 144.

Chapter 2: The Secret to Overcoming Life's Dilemmas

1. Anonymous. This work of poetic prose, in several forms, has been variously attributed and has appeared in countless print and online media.

Chapter 3: Maintaining Relationships with the People in Your Life

1. 3. This oft-quoted piece originates from a 1983 *Wall Street Journal* ad by United Technologies Corporation CEO Harry J. Gray. See Jim Borden, "How Important Are You?" Borden's Blather, June 29, 2015, https://jborden.com/2015/06/29/how-important-are-you/.

2. Julianne Holt-Lunstad et al., "Loneliness and Social Isolation as Risk Factors for Mortality: A Meta-Analytic Review," *Perspectives on Psychological Science* 10, no. 2 (March 11, 2015): 227–37. Available online at https://journals.sagepub.com/doi/10.1177/1745691614568352.

Chapter 4: How to Defuse Disharmony

1. This story is adapted from a version in Leslie B. Flynn, *You Don't Have to Go It Alone* (Denver: Accent Books, 1981), 117.
2. "Forgiveness: Your Health Depends on It," Johns Hopkins Medicine, accessed March 18, 2021, https://www.hopkinsmedicine.org/health/wellness-and-prevention/forgiveness-your-health-depends-on-it.
3. "Forgiveness."
4. Francis Bacon, "Essays or Counsels Civil and Moral," in *Bacon's Essays*, ed. F. G. Selby (London: Macmillan, 1901), 9–10.

Chapter 5: Freeing Yourself from Drama and Letting God of Envy

1. William Shakespeare, *Othello*, act 3, scene 3.
2. Quoted in Antonio Montucci, ed., *The Amusing Instructor* (London: Antonio Montucci, 1792), 125.
3. Augustine, *The Problem of Free Choice*, 1.11.22, in Augustine, *The Problem of Free Choice*, trans. Dom Mark Pontifex, Ancient Christian Writers 22 (Westminster, MD: Newman, 1955), 57–58.

Chapter 6: Maintaining Balance and Having Fun as a Grown Up

1. This quote, or variations of it, appears to have originated in a sermon by Rev. Clarence H. Wilson in 1927, though it has been attributed to a number of people since. See "How Old Would You Be if You Didn't Know How Old You Are?" Quote Investigator, https://quoteinvestigator. com/2021/08/24/how-old/.

2. Jessica Stillman, "New Stanford Study: A Positive Attitude Literally Makes Your Brain Work Better," *Inc.*, accessed March 22, 2022, https://www.inc.com/ jessica-stillman/stanford-research-attitude-matters-as-much-as-iq-in-kids-success.html.

3. Fred S. Cook, in *Quote/Unquote*, ed. Lloyd Cory (Wheaton, IL: Victor, 1977), 200. This quotation originally appeared in *Sunshine*, a monthly magazine published between 1924 and 1992.

4. Max DePree, *Leadership Is an Art* (New York: Dell Publishing, 1987), 7–10. Used by permission of Doubleday, a division of Bantam Doubleday Dell Publishing Group, Inc.

5. Jeanne Hendricks, *Afternoon* (Nashville, TN: Thomas Nelson Publishers, 1979), 103.

Chapter 7: How to Have a Joyful and Prosperous Life

1. Ella Wheeler Wilcox, "Fate," *Munsey's Magazine* 16, no. 5 (February 1897): 554.

2. See John Powell, *Why Am I Afraid to Tell You Who I Am?* (Grand Rapids: Zondervan, 1999), 30–31.

3. Powell, *Why Am I Afraid?*, 31.

4. Powell, *Why Am I Afraid?*, 32.

5. Powell, *Why Am I Afraid?*, 33.

6. Powell, *Why Am I Afraid?*, 35–36.

7. Howard Taylor and Mary G. Taylor, *Hudson Taylor's Spiritual Secret*, Moody Classics (Chicago: Moody, 1999), 153.

8. Lexico, s.v. "attitude," https://www.lexico.com/en/definition/attitude.

9. From *Good Reading*, in *Quote/Unquote*, comp. Lloyd Cory (Wheaton, IL: Victor, 1977), 23.

10. Isaac Watts, "When I Survey the Wondrous Cross," in *The Psalms, Hymns, and Spiritual Songs by the Rev. Isaac Watts*, new ed. (London: W. Baynes, 1817), 610.

11. Quoted in Warren W. Wiersbe, *The Bible Exposition Commentary: New Testament* (Colorado Springs: Victor, 1989), 2:73.

12. D. Martyn Lloyd-Jones, *The Life of Joy: An Exposition of Philippians 1 and 2* (Grand Rapids, MI: Baker, 1989), 142–43.

13. Wilcox, "Fate," 554.

Conclusion

1. Henry David Thoreau, *Walden* (New York: Thomas Y. Crowell, 1910), 427.

2. Robert Ballard, "A Long Last Look at Titanic," *National Geographic* 170, no. 6 (December 1986): 698–705.

3. Benjamin Franklin, at the signing of the Declaration of Independence (July 4, 1776), cited in John Bartlett, *Familiar Quotations*, 9th ed. (Boston: Little, Brown, and Co., 1894), 362.

From the Publisher

GREAT BOOKS

ARE EVEN BETTER WHEN THEY'RE SHARED!

Help other readers find this one:

- Post a review at your favorite online bookseller

- Post a picture on a social media account and share why you enjoyed it

- Send a note to a friend who would also love it—or better yet, give them a copy

Thanks for reading!

ABOUT THE AUTHOR

CHARLES R. SWINDOLL IS THE FOUNDER AND SEN-ior pastor-teacher of Stonebriar Community Church in Frisco, Texas. But Chuck's listening audience extends far beyond a local church body, as Insight for Living airs on major Christian radio markets around the world. Chuck's extensive writing ministry has also served the body of Christ worldwide, and his leadership as president and now chancellor emeritus of Dallas Theological Seminary has helped prepare and equip a new generation of men and women for ministry. Chuck and his wife, Cynthia, his partner in life and ministry, have four grown children, ten grandchildren, and seven great-grandchildren.